**1939**
A RETROSPECT FORTY YEARS AFTER

*(for*

# 1939,
# A RETROSPECT FORTY
# YEARS AFTER)

Proceedings of a Conference
held at the University of Surrey
27 October 1979

*Edited by*
## Roy Douglas
*Reader*
*General Studies Department*
*University of Surrey*

1983
Archon Books

*First published 1983 in the UK by*
THE MACMILLAN PRESS LTD
*London and Basingstoke*
*and in the USA by*
*Archon Books, an imprint of*
*The Shoe String Press, Inc.*
*995 Sherman Avenue*
*Hamden, Connecticut 06514*

ISBN   0-208-02020-9

*Printed in Hong Kong*

---

**Library of Congress Cataloging in Publication Data**

---

Main entry under title:

1939, a retrospect forty years after.

   Bibliography: p.
   Includes index.
   1. World War, 1939–1945 — Causes — Congresses.
2. World War, 1939–1945 — Historiography — Congresses.
3. Europe — History — 1918–1945 — Congresses. I. Douglas,
Roy, 1924–     . II. Title: 1939, a retrospect 40 years
after.
D741.A14   1983   940.53′11                    82–24481
ISBN   0-208-02020-9

---

# Contents

# Acknowledgements

The Modern History Group is organised through the General Studies Department of the University of Surrey. The editor, who also acted as chairman of the conference, gratefully acknowledges the help of the Head of the Department, Mr J. P. Freyne, and the members of the secretarial staff, plus the members of the action committee for this conference, namely, Mark Ashworth, Peter Beardsley, Professor Frank Healey, Frank Moles, Mrs Morag Morris, Bertram Pockney and Professor Keith Puttick.

R.D.

# Notes on the Contributors

**Dr Roy Douglas**, Reader at the University of Surrey, was formerly a biologist and later turned to history. His books include *The History of the Liberal Party 1895–1970* (1971), *Land, People and Politics* (1976), *In the Year of Munich* (1977), *The Advent of War 1939–40* (1979), *From War to Cold War 1942–48* (1981) and *New Alliances 1940–41* (1982).

**Dr Józef Garliński** obtained his first degree in 1942 from the clandestine University of Warsaw and his PhD from the London School of Economics. He was active in the Polish Home Army during the war, and spent two years in German concentration camps. His books include *Poland, S.O.E. and the Allies* (1963), *Fighting Auschwitz* (1975), *Hitler's Last Weapons* (1978), *Intercept: Secrets of the 'Enigma' War* (1979) and *The Swiss Corridor* (1981). He is currently working on a further book, *Poland in the Second World War*.

**Professor Douglas Johnson**, FR Hist S, has been Professor of French History at University College, London, since 1968. His publications include *Guizot: Aspects of French History, 1787–1874* (1963), *France and the Dreyfus Affair* (1966), *France* (1969), *Concise History of France* (1970) and *The French Revolution* (1970).

**Dr Lothar Kettenacker** was born in 1939 and studied at the Universities of Frankfurt/Main, Munich and Oxford. His PhD, from Frankfurt, was published as *Nationalsozialistische Volksturmpolitik im Elsass* in Stuttgart, 1973, and in French from Strasbourg in 1976. He has been Secretary of the Anglo-German Group of Historians since 1972, and Deputy Director of the German Historical Institute in London since 1975. He has edited several books and published various articles on National Socialism, Anglo-German relations and, in particular, British postwar planning for Germany, on which he will be bringing out a book in 1983.

**Margot Light** is a Lecturer in Russian and Soviet Studies in the Department of Linguistic and International Studies at the University of Surrey. She teaches Russian language, Soviet history, Soviet foreign policy and international relations. Her research interests include international relations theory, Soviet theories of international relations and conflict analysis.

**Dr A. J. P. Taylor,** Hon DCL (New Brunswick), D Univ York, D Litt (Bristol), Hon D Litt (Warwick), Hon D Litt (Manchester), FBA from 1956 until his resignation in 1980, Hon Fellow, Magdalen College, Oxford, Hon Fellow, Oriel College, Oxford, is author of a great many books and other publications, including *The Habsburg Monarchy 1815–1918* (1941), *The Course of German History* (1945), *From Napoleon to Stalin* (1950), *The Struggle for Mastery in Europe 1848–1918* (1954), *Bismarck* (1955), *The Trouble-Makers* (1957), *The Origins of the Second World War* (1961), *English History 1914–45* (1965), *From Sarajevo to Potsdam* (1966), *War by Timetable* (1969), *Beaverbrook* (1972), *The Second World War* (1975) and *How Wars Begin* (1979).

**Professor Donald Cameron Watt**, FR Hist S, Stevenson Professor of International History at the University of London since 1981, took his degrees from Oxford. He was assistant editor of the published *Documents on German Foreign Policy 1918–1945*, and is author of a considerable number of books and other publications, including *Britain and the Suez Crisis* (1956), *Personalities and Politics* (1965), *History of the World in the Twentieth Century*, Part 1 (1967), *Hitler's Mein Kampf* (1969), *Too Serious a Business* (1975) and *European Armed Forces and the Coming of the Second World War* (1975).

# Some Important Dates

| | |
|---|---|
| 30 January 1933 | Adolf Hitler becomes Chancellor of Germany. |
| 2 October 1935 | Italian invasion of Abyssinia. |
| 7 March 1936 | German reoccupation of Rhineland. |
| 12 March 1938 | German troops invade Austria. |
| 30 September 1938 | Munich agreement. |
| 14 March 1939 | Slovakia declares independence. |
| 15 March 1939 | German troops occupy Bohemia and Moravia. |
| 22 March 1939 | Lithuania cedes Memel to Germany. |
| 28 March 1939 | Franco announces that he is in control of all provinces in Spain. |
| 31 March 1939 | British guarantee of Poland announced. |
| 7 April 1939 | Italian invasion of Albania. |
| 4 May 1939 | Molotov becomes Soviet Foreign Minister in succession to Litvinov. |
| 21 August 1939 | Announcement that Non-Aggression Pact will be concluded between Germany and Russia. |
| 23 August 1939 | Signature of Non-Aggression Pact. |
| 25 August 1939 | Anglo-Polish Treaty signed. Postponement of German invasion of Poland, planned for 26 August. |
| 1 September 1939 | German invasion of Poland. |
| 2 September 1939 | Growing uncertainty about French intentions. Italian attempt to secure conference. House of Commons demonstration in favour of declaration of war. (Midnight) Cabinet decision to issue ultimatum to Germany. |
| 3 September 1939 | (9 a.m.) British ultimatum to Germany. (11.15 a.m.) Chamberlain announces that Britain is at war with Germany. (5 p.m.) France at war with Germany. |

| | |
|---|---|
| 3–10 September 1939 | British Dominions (except Eire) declare war on Germany. |
| 17 September 1939 | Soviet invasion of Poland. |
| 27 September 1939 | Surrender of Warsaw. |
| 29 September 1939 | Soviet–German Treaty on partitioning of Poland. |
| 29 September–<br>10 October 1939 | Soviet 'agreements' with Estonia, Latvia and Lithuania result in grant of Soviet bases in all three countries, and in Wilno (Vilna) passing to Lithuania. |

# Introduction

**Roy Douglas**

The chapters in this book have been edited from lectures delivered at a one-day conference, held at the University of Surrey on 27 October 1979. The theme was 'Forty Years After'; the object was to look at events which took place about the time of the outbreak of the Second World War from the angles of the five countries which were involved during the first month: the United Kingdom, France, Poland, Germany and Russia.

The interval of forty years was chosen deliberately. British official documents are subject to a 'thirty-year rule' – that is, they become available for public inspection after thirty years unless there are special reasons for keeping them secret. It is true that selections from these documents were published long ago in the *Documents on British Foreign Policy*;[1] but other material – such as many Foreign Office papers, and collections of private papers from Neville Chamberlain and Viscount (later Earl) Halifax[2] – has only become available much more recently. While the impression presented by these new documents is not wildly different from that of the older selection, important new side-lights are certainly cast, and more depth is given to the picture. By adding ten more years to the thirty, we allow scholars reasonable time to look over those documents, publish their conclusions and criticise each other's interpretations. British private documents, and the official documents of other countries, are subject to different rules – some become available sooner, some later, and some (like many of the Soviet documents which we would particularly like to see) not at all. Forty years after events, however, it usually becomes possible to piece together the evidence which has been disclosed and produce a moderately complete picture. No doubt it would be convenient, from some points of view, to wait for the fiftieth anniversary; but there would be substantially fewer people who could recall their own

1

impressions of the period and check those remembered impressions against what scholars think happened.

At this conference, and in this small volume, an attempt has been made to present as many disparate outlooks as possible. It goes without saying that neither the contributors nor the editor take responsibility for each other's views. It is hoped that these essays will encourage examination of historical problems from unfamiliar angles; for most people are naturally disposed to see past events from the standpoint of their own experience, their own nations, their own philosophy, their own estimate of what was to play the most vital part in future events.

If there is one consistent impression which is brought home from these varied, and in places contradictory, pictures of the situation in August – September 1939, it is the appalling character of the choices which every one of the five countries was forced to make. When we ask ourselves today, forty years after, what the governments of those countries *should* have done at the time, we still find it inordinately difficult to give a satisfactory answer, and unless we are very careful indeed we find ourselves answering very different questions – such as what they should have done in 1936 or even earlier.

Most people today would assess actions of the late 1930s by the test: was this behaviour the best way of destroying Nazism and containing German expansion? This test was by no means equally obvious at the time. In many parts of the world there seemed to be much more to fear from other states with known or suspected expansionist aspirations – a group including Italy, Japan, the Soviet Union and even relatively small countries like Hungary. Even within a single country there could be massive geographical variations. A Soviet citizen in Leningrad or an American in New York had good reason for apprehension at the rise of Germany; a Soviet citizen in Vladivostok or an American is San Francisco had much more cause to be worried about Japan. Perhaps a Pole in Warsaw was mainly fearful of Germany, while a Pole in Lwów was more fearful of Russia. Even within Britain, the perceived dangers changed markedly during the late 1930s. Until the end of 1937, there was more agitation about Italy than Germany; by the autumn of 1938 Italy was generally treated as only a minor irritation by comparison with Germany. The one thing which was absolutely clear was that those countries which were on the whole satisfied with the international status quo ('peace-loving countries', as they rather smugly described themselves) could not hold back all the actual or potential 'revisionists' simultaneously. Either the 'revisionists' must be played off against each other, or else the other countries must establish some kind of association with certain 'revisionists' in opposition to others.

Why France or Russia or Poland should have been especially worried about German expansion in Europe is obvious enough. All of those countries lay on the likely German line of march; and in all three cases later events would show that the worst fears were justified. With Britain it was different. There had once been a considerable amount of altruistic sympathy for Germany – not least on the political 'left' – which had little parallel in other European countries. Many people were disposed to look at Hitler's known or believed territorial aspirations on their individual merits, rather than as parts of a very dangerous and sinister programme. No doubt the continental European, appalled at the threat to his own country, would have observed with some heat that Britain could afford this Olympian detachment because of her geographical security. The only claim which the Nazis made against Britain in the run-up period to the war was for the pre-1914 German colonies; and even that claim was more or less forgotten after 1937. The real risk which Germany posed to Britain was that if she became supreme on the continent – and particularly if she somehow acquired a large fleet in the process – Britain might be left alone and friendless to face an irresistible challenge. The British, however, are proud of their empirical approach, and tend not to take very seriously long-term arguments which turn on several imponderables. Some of the contributors throw light on the process by which Britain came to look away from the obvious and direct threats to her Empire which were posed by Italy and Japan, and towards the much more indirect threat from Germany. Perhaps the event which finally convinced most people in Britain that Germany really was their main enemy was the seizure of Prague on 15 March 1939. The message which nearly everybody took very clearly was that this represented a total violation of what Hitler had agreed at Munich. The problem was not just that Germany was strong and would drive a very hard bargain; but that no bargain which Hitler made would be kept if it did not suit his purpose. It was thus pointless to conclude any kind of agreement with him; the only choice facing Britain was whether to acquiesce in Hitler taking whatever he wanted – or, alternatively, to decide that if he exceeded certain limits, Britain would go to war with him.

Thus by the spring of 1939 most people in Britain, France and Poland, and also (for the time being) most people in the Soviet Union, had probably decided that there was much to be said for holding candles to various other devils in order to exorcise Nazi Germany.

Britain had long avoided any commitment to countries which were inaccessible by sea. Her brief and highly ambiguous commitment to Czechoslovakia looked like being an exception; but the real change in foreign policy was made by the guarantee to Poland issued at the end of March 1939, which was solidified into a bilateral treaty on 25 August – just after the Russo-German Non-Aggression Pact was announced. The original intention of the British Government when the Germans marched into Prague, however, had been something quite different. They had sought to engineer a 'Grand Alliance' against further German expansion, which should incorporate at least Britain, France, Poland and Russia, and perhaps others as well. This approach ran into early difficulties; but the circumstances which actually produced the guarantee to Poland were astonishing. When the British Government was still reeling from the destruction of Czechoslovakia, some very tenuous evidence appeared, suggesting that Germany was poised to coerce Poland: perhaps to extract an unequal treaty from the Poles, perhaps to invade the country. In all ordinary circumstances, such news would have produced a flurry of minutes in the Foreign Office and perhaps a brief discussion in the Cabinet, but nothing more. This time everybody from the Prime Minister downwards was in such an acute state of nerves that the Government took the evidence seriously. They decided that if something was not done immediately, people were likely to wake up one morning soon and learn that Hitler had struck – when it would be too late. So a 'guarantee' was offered to Poland. If Germany attacked, and the Poles fought back, then Britain would go to war with Germany. The Poles accepted the guarantee and on 31 March it was announced in the House of Commons. The MPs and the press mostly welcomed the news; and so, to all appearances, did most ordinary people. Probably a great many of them neither knew nor cared what the exact implications of the guarantee were – still less how it would be honoured if matters came to the crunch. The one thing of interest was that apparently Hitler was going to be 'stopped'.

When the new guarantee was added to various existing treaties, the overall effect was to make it likely that Britain, France and Poland would soon find themselves as allies in a war against Germany – with or without various other countries participating on one side or the other. Insofar as it was possible to make any predictions about the military situation in event of war, however, the picture was not very encouraging. The question was therefore raised: how could the alliance be strengthened by accession of other allies? If that could not be done, then how could the existing allies co-operate to the best effect?

Allies never have identical aims and interests. However close and honest an alliance may be, any country would rather see a thousand soldiers of its ally killed than a thousand of its own. In practice, allies usually have a great many more complex reservations about interest than that. This looks like a statement of the blindingly obvious, and perhaps it is; yet it is curious how often such facts are forgotten, and allies deeply resent each other's behaviour when interests begin to diverge. In the course of this present study, we shall receive insight about practical difficulties presented to statesmen who sought to make the existing alliance militarily effective – and the even greater difficulties which they encountered when they sought to extend it in a way which might permanently deter Germany from going to war.

Our study will finally require us to look at matters from the German angle. This is the most difficult, and in one sense the most important of all to understand. It is today axiomatic, and justly axiomatic, in all lands, that the Nazi regime was a monstrous tyranny whose policy brought ruin and desolation on everybody it touched, and not least upon the German people themselves. Yet, forty years ago, a great many people in Germany were willing to set their lives at peril to ensure its success, and a great many people in other lands were willing to hitch the destinies of their own countries to the same cause. To understand the situation in 1939, it is necessary to appreciate why this was so.

## NOTES AND REFERENCES

1. *Documents on British Foreign Policy 1919–1939*, edited by E.L. Woodward and R. Butler, Third Series (London, 1949 *et seq.*).
2. Neville Chamberlain papers, University of Birmingham Library. Viscount (later Earl) Halifax papers: FO 800/309–328 at Public Record Office, Kew, Surrey, and 'Hickleton papers', Churchill College, Cambridge.

# 1 · Setting the Scene

## Donald Cameron Watt

The forty years which followed the outbreak of war in 1939 have been years of historiography: forty years in which there has grown up in Britain what one can only describe as a historical industry, on the origins of the Second World War. It is interesting that there is no such industry in the United States. It is also remarkable how little work has been done so far in France to parallel the work that has been done in Britain on the period of appeasement; while the Soviet Union's historians have not been allowed to change their minds at all over the intervening period. It is true that in the 1960s there was a movement among Soviet historians which argued that in the light of the de-Stalinisation process they ought to be able to say things about Stalin's judgement which were somewhat less than reverential; but the members of this group were out-manoeuvred by their old-style Stalinist colleagues, and most of them are now out of a job or in exile. Their most prominent member, V. Nekrich, is in the West. What happened to their assistants, their graduate students and so on, we of course don't know. The only thing one could say now about the Soviet historians is that they are today allowed to admit – in front of Western audiences at least – that there were other participants in the Second World War on the Allied side, apart from the Soviet Red Army.

The historiography of the Second World War was given an immense encouragement by the events of the Nuremberg trials. The decision to try the surviving members of the Nazi leadership, together with a rather curious assembly of other individuals, on war-crime charges, fixed a 'conspiratorial' theory of the origin of the Second World War. American opinion wished to date the origins of this conspiracy to the foundations of the Nazi Party; but it was eventually decided to base the prosecution of the conspirators on their part in the audience to Hitler's speech of 5

6

November 1937. This speech is known as the Hossbach speech, after the gentleman who eventually wrote down his own recollections of part of it. The 'conspiratorial theory' was very much enhanced by the appearance shortly after Nuremberg of the first volume of Winston Churchill's memoirs of the Second World War.[1] The industry, however, was well established in Britain before Nuremberg, indeed it was flourishing during the Second World War. It had then a very strong political element: the search for 'guilty men'. This search was launched both on left and right. Michael Foot, Frank Owen and others, masquerading under various Latin names, began it by writing short books which were published by Gollancz and the Left Book Club.[2] For at least a decade after the Second World War, the search for villains and defendants was continued by the right-wing historians who had supported Winston Churchill in the 1930s: of whom Sir Lewis Namier was the most distinguished, though by no means alone. Few, if any, of this generation now survive. They execrated appeasement, attacking the British Government of the time for a variety of sins. One cannot help feeling that lack of masculinity was the strongest element in their indictment. These historians represented what we would now call the 'spirit of masculinity' in politics. The British Government was indicted for not standing up, for not having certain obvious masculine protruberances. They were dismissed in terms reminiscent of the old-style form master's reports at the end of term, like 'Could do better'. 'Despite the habitual levity of his dispositon, inevitably gravitates to the bottom' and so on.

In the 1950s I began as a junior, assisting the process of editing captured German documents, which were being published by the Foreign Office. When I left that task and came to London, I was told there was no point in working on the history of that period. It was all known and that was that. Indeed, for about six or seven years it was very difficult, if not impossible, to get anything published in England on the subject — at least in the learned journals. This spell was broken towards the end of the 1950s by the appearance of Alan Taylor's *Origins of the Second World War*:[3] a perverse work in some ways, but one which uncovered — with uncomfortable accuracy — the defects in what was then the orthodox, accepted view.

In the 1950s and early 1960s, the bulk of the work that was being done by the next generation of historians in Britain can best be described as neo-Conservative. It involved the re-evaluation of the 1930s and even the 1920s. This was the era which saw the production of massive biographies of Baldwin, of attempts to reassess Neville Chamberlain and so on. Behind their work there lay two other developments. The first of these lines of development was exemplified by the work of a number of official historians in the Cabinet Office. There was enough in their work and in that of the neo-Conservatives to show that the orthodox Churchillian indictment of British policy in the 1930s rested on a very wide range of misunderstandings as to what the preoccupations of the British Government of that period were. This approach appealed to people in the 1950s, who were currently witnessing the perpetual excess of British commitments over British resources in the external world. The shock of the Suez campaign — which only underlined this — was reflected in the work which was to follow, in which the policies of the 1930s were defended by men who pointed out that similar discrepancies between commitments and resources had existed in the earlier period.

The second line of development characteristic of the 1950s and early 1960s was first signalled by the appearance of some spiritual successors to the Michael Foot — Frank Owen group. Two young men (as they were then) — Martin Gilbert and Richard Gott — wrote a book called *The Appeasers*.[4] Indeed, I think it was the appearance of *The Appeasers* which convinced nearly everybody that that particular line of attack no longer had any validity in it. Richard Gott deserted such studies for journalism, and the search for revolutions to back in Latin America and elsewhere, through the columns of the *Guardian*. Martin Gilbert stayed, and has now become the biographer of Winston Churchill; but in his second book, *Roots of Appeasement*,[5] and in the second edition of Alan Taylor's *Origins of the Second World War*,[6] that line of development took a new twist. In these books were found, for the first time, attempts to defend the 'appeasers' on the grounds that they represented, in Alan Taylor's words, 'the best forces in Britain'. They represented what he had already described as 'the alternative tradition of British foreign policy': those who felt that war was the wrong way of solving international disputes; those who believed that there was no dispute that could not be mediated, provided that men of good will could be got around a table; those who felt that it was distortions in the system of international relations itself that produced war, and so on.

In the most recent developments of British historiography, there has been particular concentration on the strategic factor in British policy. This has underlined the arguments that were advanced in the 1950s and early 1960s about the disparity between British resources and British commitments. There has been a whole new series of books studying this in relation to different parts of the world. That investigation has now shifted to an analysis of other elements in the British policy-making bureaucracy. Such recent books involve a study of rearmament and what went wrong with that. They include a book produced earlier this year by George Peden of the University of Bristol, on the role of the Treasury in appeasement.[7] There have also been studies of the role of the Dominions and other parts of the English-speaking world.

As a result of the work of this school, it is now possible to detect a belated echo of this historiographical interest in America. For a long time, whatever little work appeared in the United States about this period of British policy, consisted very largely of attempts to demonstrate the truth of the Gilbert and Gott thesis. These rather peculiar works included one which actually said that it was all the fault of the British aristocracy, which felt its position under threat, and was therefore inclined towards Germany rather than the Soviet Union. One has only to think of the Conservative Cabinet of the day to see how wrong this was. Neville Chamberlain was the son of a screw manufacturer who went into small arms; and most of his Cabinet belonged to what one could describe as the industrial high bourgeoisie rather than the aristocracy. Indeed, there were many more aristocratic elements in the Churchillian group opposed to appeasement than there were in Neville Chamberlain's Cabinet. But now one can see among American historians the beginning of an attempt to adapt this reevaluation of British policy to America, and to regard the policies of President Roosevelt with somewhat less than the adulation which had so long been a feature of the dominant New Deal school of historiography in the United States.

There is one further development of significance. This is an attempt to return to the idea (very current in the 1930s) that what was happening in Europe was not a struggle for mastery between European nations, but an ideological struggle, a European civil war. Perhaps the best statement of this has been in a book by a Hungarian historian who is now in the United States, John Lukacs, entitled *The Last European War*,[8] which studies the

period between 1939 and 1941, but also goes into the prewar
period. It raises two issues: if the Second World War was a
*European* war, what did it settle? And if it was a European *civil*
war, occurring within some kind of *civitas*, then what was that
European society which was at loggerheads with itself? For the
most obvious thing that the Second World War did was to destroy
the European position of domination in the world, which had
already been badly shaken by the First World War. It led the way
for the super powers to meet in the centre of Europe; and it was
followed by the collapse of the European colonial empires. It
divided Europe so much that when we use the word 'Europe' now
we generally mean Western Europe, and exclude the Eastern
European satellites of the Soviet Union.

Yet we may fairly reflect that the war did in truth settle
something else. It ensured that what is variously called totalit-
arianism, fascism or authoritarianism lost its appeal as a desirable
form of government in Western Europe. Over the last thousand
years or more, one can see in European politics a struggle between
systems of government essentially based on the idea of authority
from above, acquiesced in by the mass of the people, and
government which relied on participation by various elements –
interest groups and so on – among the people. Even the Gaullist
experiments in France do not vitiate the view that the idea of
authority from above has received, at any rate for the next
generation or two, a total defeat in the Western part of Europe.
That fact represents a remarkable gain, at least for European
humanity, and perhaps for the rest of the world too. If this view is
correct, then the crucial events of the 1930s should be seen as a
struggle within a political entity, Europe, rather than a struggle
between the component parts of Europe.

In any event, the idea that the Second World War was
essentially a European civil war raised the important question:
how do we define 'Europe'? We can see it in terms of geography,
or we can see it in terms of geo-politics. If we regard Europe as a
cultural entity, then where are its boundaries? Much more
important, where did people of the time consider them to lie? It
seems to me that there were two alternative sets of ideas in
people's minds at the time about 'Europe'.

The first idea is what one might call the 'Little Europe' fallacy.
On that view, a particular country could opt out and declare,
'We are not a part of Europe'. This 'isolationist' idea was, of

course, strongest in Britain. A substantial number of people in the 1920s and early 1930s manifestly did not regard Britain as part of Europe. On its fringes, if you like! Some of them thought that Britain was a mid-Atlantic state – as though in some way or other it had been towed a thousand miles westward and dumped in the neighbourhood of the Sargasso Sea. Others were far more concerned with the protection of British possessions overseas and of the Dominions, and with the threat from Japan, than they were with any threat from Europe. This view attracted prominent members of policy-forming groups, such as Lord Hankey, Secretary both of the Cabinet and of the Committee of Imperial Defence.

This desire to withdraw from Europe, however, was not peculiar to Britain. It was evinced in other European countries from time to time. In 1936, Belgium withdrew from its alliances; while in 1938 a grouping of neutralist states signed the Declaration of Copenhagen. Unfortunately only two out of all the signatories of the Declaration of Copenhagen were actually able to realise their hopes. Contracting out takes more than an act of will by the would-be contractor: it also requires good will from those from whom you are trying to contract out; and that good will was not forthcoming. Nor, indeed, did the desire to withdraw from Europe disappear when the war was over. It was witnessed again in the attitude which many Germans took when the ideas of German conscription and German participation in the Cold War were bruited during the 1950s.

The second idea is a compensating error – what we might call the 'Greater Europe' fallacy. The authors of the system set up by the Treaty of Versailles thought they were establishing a system for the whole of the world. The language, the conceptual framework, the ethos to which the authors of the League of Nations appealed, was the idea of world peace. In practice, the assumptions which they held in their minds turned on the idea of *European* peace. The Treaty of Versailles, and the system of international security set up by the Covenant of the League of Nations, would have been very effective in preventing the kind of war that broke out in Europe in 1914. It was, as we all know, a great deal less successful in dealing with the wars which actually flared up in the 1930s – first in the Far East, then in the Mediterranean and only belatedly, at the end of the decade, in Europe. All the will and the stuffing had gone out of its members.

By contrast, in 1914 'Europe' had meant 'the world' for most purposes. In the late Lord Keynes's *Economic Consequences of the Peace*, there is a superb passage which describes the nature of the prewar world: how, sitting in one's rooms in London, one could order and buy shares and bonds in cities all over the world and invest wherever one wanted; how one could go to one's bank and draw sufficient supply of sovereigns or gold, or even the money of foreign countries, and travel wherever one wished – with the possible exception of Tsarist Russia.[9] This might be described as a Harrods-eye view of the world, because it was only available if one could afford to patronise that haunt of the upper bourgeoisie. But it was, nevertheless, something perfectly genuine. It may be contrasted with the system prevailing in the Europe of 1925: a Europe which had to some extent solved its own problems, but had solved them on the basis of an economic system relying on frequent injections of American money. That system in its turn was to break down from 1929 onwards, as soon as American money ceased to flow. What was brought out both before and after 1929 was the impoverishment of Europe, and the destruction of the pre-1914 system: whether one is thinking of the social system, the political system or the economic order.

The peace settlement of 1919 was unstable for a variety of reasons. It started from the belief that economic sanctions would probably restrain an aggressor. Yet the only would-be aggressor who has ever been restrained by economic sanctions was the British Government, at the time of Suez. If economic sanctions failed, then it was believed that a threat to make war universal would deter the aggressor: fifty nations against one, as it was said at the time of the Abyssinian dispute. In practice, many of the fifty were very reluctant to get involved. This appeared to vindicate the argument which the British Chiefs of Staff had been maintaining since 1923. The major League of Nations powers would have to increase their military armament very considerably – because, under the terms of the Covenant, they might find themselves called upon to intervene by force anywhere in the world, and without prior preparation, at the dictate of the League itself. In other words, it added still further obligations to the traditional British commitment to defend her own territory, to defend the territory of her allies and to defend international sea routes. The underlying assumption of the League of Nations was that large forces would be available to defend its own system of security.

Thus rearmament became the order of the day, and British Governments of the 1930s came to see that they were even less well prepared to deal with three potential enemies in three widely separated parts of the world than they had been in 1914. Britain had a smaller navy and a less effective army. She had an air force, it was true; but this air force was only good for deterring France. It was in no position to bomb other states – certainly not Germany – until 1941 or so.

But the peace settlement was not only unstable because of these intellectual contradictions in the Treaty of Versailles and in the Covenant of the League of Nations. It was unstable because the events of the First World War, and the revolutions which followed it, had created permanent instabilities in Europe – especially in Germany and France and throughout Eastern Europe.

This brings us to enquire as to the nature of the society within which the European civil war raged. It was characterised by several features. First, it was governed by a political system and an agreement on the rules of the game by which that system was operated. This, of course, does not mean that the rules were always observed – any more than people playing football always observe the rules of that game. Thus the second feature of the society was that it had to provide some kind of mechanism by which people violating those rules could be penalised. The third element of the European society was that it contained inter-linked social élites. The most obvious of these was composed of people who were dominant within the structures of the individual states, by virtue of either their social or their political position. Those dominant élites were paralleled, during the 1920s and 1930s, by dissidents within each society; and between those dissidents there also existed links. The links between dissidents on the 'right' were not very important, at any rate until after the advent of Hitler to power in Germany. There were much more important links between dissidents on the 'left', between the international revolutionaries and between the international non-revolutionary 'left'.

The nature of these links between dissidents on the left calls for some digression; for those links were to be exploited by the Soviet Union from 1934 onwards in its advocacy of 'Popular Fronts'. The idea of Popular Fronts was that the forces of 'progress' – intellectuals, the working class and so on – should come together in a union against those who were depriving them of their rights or impeding them on their march towards participation. This idea was fostered originally by Willi Münzenberg a German Communist who had had Lenin's ear: a man who had been politically active at the time when the organisation of Communist parties was being taken over and dominated by Russians, to the disadvantage and destruction of most of the parties of the European 'left'. Münzenberg was later allowed by Moscow to preach the doctrine of unity of the left against those who sought to challenge it. Through the International Workers' Help movement and through all the variety of 'Fronts' he was able to spawn from it – and through the extraordinary press, publishing and film empire he built up in Germany – he was able to mitigate the destructive work of the Russian Bolshevik leaders on the European left. When he was expelled from Germany – or escaped from Germany – in 1933, he tried to build up a similar centre in Paris and with a good deal of success. It was from this base that the idea of the Popular Front was launched. Already, in 1932, he had begun to set up international committees to fight Fascism, with the usual 'front board' of distinguished left-wing writers and others. The Popular Front movement proved its strength at the time of the Europe-wide movement to aid the Spanish Government during the Spanish Civil War; but it fell victim to the purges which Stalin launched in Russia and which were to spread to the rest of the European left-wing movements. The Popular Front movement ended with the signature of the Nazi–Soviet pact, and the elimination of the leadership of the European revolutionary left – wherever Russian agents could get hold of them. The Popular Front movement was no longer useful to the Soviet leaders, now that the Soviet Union had withdrawn from Europe.

There is a lot to be said for the view that the Popular Front movement had never been seen by the Soviet leadership as more than a holding operation – a means of keeping the wars they saw coming away from the Soviet Union. This they did by playing on and backing and encouraging the various forces of liberalism, social democracy and revolutionary democracy (if one may call it that), within Europe itself. But events of 1939 destroyed all ideas of the Popular Front and the French Communist Party – the most Stalinist of all – helped to sap the morale of the French army, and did its bit (though one should not exaggerate that bit) in producing the collapse of France in the summer of 1940.

The United States also withdrew largely from Europe, though for different reasons and in a different manner from the Soviet

Union. The Treaty of Versailles failed to secure a two-thirds majority in Senate; but during the 1920s America moved reluctantly back to concern with Europe, in matters both of economics and of security. Under Franklin Roosevelt, the United States took itself away from Europe again, and in 1933 the last attempt on the part of the European states to solve their economic problems collectively was torpedoed by the action of the American Government. From 1933 to 1937, Roosevelt and the American people languished in a renewed isolationism from Europe. Neutrality laws were passed, designed to prevent America from ever being drawn into European war again – thus penalising countries which wished to call the resources of American industry to their aid. This policy made the British Government much more reluctant to take a strong line until its own rearmament programme had begun to pay off in Europe. From 1937 onwards, Roosevelt himself began to move away from this position; but his movement was slow and tentative, and American opinion up until 1939 (perhaps even until 1940) tended to regard what was happening in Europe as a kind of spectator sport – one in which the Europeans were living up (or rather down) to the worst expectations of Americans. The British ruling class was seen to be behaving with the kind of moral cowardice which, the Americans had come to persuade themselves, was characteristic of them. Thus the position of leader in the world of masculinity was considered to have passed to the United States.

When one looks at the efforts which were being made by the British Government at that time to control events in Europe, it becomes apparent that the idea of a European security system without the United States or the Soviet Union was now uppermost in the thoughts of Neville Chamberlain. He had not ruled out participation of those two entirely, but he thought that the cost of bringing them in was too high for Britain to pay, save in the last resort.

So far as Europe in the 1930s was concerned, America was a country of fantasy. In the minds of some British– and, indeed, some French – statesmen in 1940, it was the last and ultimate goddess from the machine who could be called in to put things right. Georges Bonnet, who was French Foreign Minister at the beginning of the Second World War, had originally been appointed because it was believed that his previous experience of America enabled him to play the American card; but it was not a card which he found up his sleeve when he wanted to play it. One finds the final expression of this view of America in Paul Reynaud's appeal to the United States to declare war, in the summer of 1940: a measure of his despair, rather than of his grasp of political realities. Churchill also saw America in that light. He took the view that Chamberlain's rejection of Roosevelt's message in January 1938 was the most extraordinary thing he had ever done. I suspect Churchill had never read the message properly, for it did not ever bear the interpretation he put upon it. Chamberlain himself briefly saw America as the ultimate saviour of Europe. In the first three months of 1939, he came to think that the much more bellicose noises then emerging from President Roosevelt were playing their part in restraining Hitler. It is arguable that this view of America has something to do with Chamberlain's idea, in the first three months of 1939, that he saw peace on the horizon. That impression seems to have convinced him that appeasement was paying off; that the Americans were becoming more involved; and that this was having its effect on Hitler. He was soon to be disillusioned.

All the British Government wanted from America and from the Soviet Union was this kind of support. The price which would be exacted for closer American or Soviet participation was simply too high. If the British Government took this view about America, then how much more did the states of Eastern Europe take the same view of the Soviet Union, which was the only country able to help them if the Germans really attacked.

In any event, all hopes of securing the right measure of American and Russian support were dashed when the Germans marched into Prague in March 1939. The situation was not improved when Roosevelt sent a message to Hitler at Easter, inviting the Führer to pledge himself not to attack a list of states which included places as far away as Iraq. Hitler was able to score off Roosevelt in his reply; and the correspondence certainly removed any fears which the German Government might have had about active American intervention.

After Hitler had marched into Prague, the British tried to set up a system in Eastern Europe which would draw the line on further German advances – threatening them with war and Soviet invasion if they overstepped it. This effort was turned, under Soviet pressure, into negotiations for an alliance involving the Soviet Union. These negotiations also broke down – as much as anything because the Polish and Romanian Governments, and the social strata on which their power rested, felt that to call in the Soviet Union would be as bad as calling in the Germans. Either way, they were finished – the independence of their countries was at an end – their attempt to occupy some kind of independent position between their more mighty neighbours was through. And, of course, they were right – as the events of 1944–5 were to show.

The European security system which had been set up in the interwar years broke down bit by bit; but its disintegration evidently began between 1929 and 1933 when there was no more American money and the European economy collapsed. Thereafter, from his advent to power in 1933 down to the German–Soviet pact of 1939, Hitler sought gradually to free himself from any anxieties about the east. This left his way open for rectification of the position of German vulnerability in the west, which had been set up by Versailles.

France, Britain and the Soviet Union had all apparently had some alternatives open to them besides acquiescence in the German advance. The French tried to reach agreement with Italy and the Soviet Union. This attempt broke down because the price the Italians exacted was the setting up of an empire in Ethiopia; while the Soviet Union was only prepared to go so far in furtherance of French wishes. The British attempted to mediate possible areas of contention with Germany – at least until the British rearmament effort had begun to pay off – but they found Hitler one move ahead of them every time. The Soviet Union's attempt to set up a collective security system based on the Popular Fronts also suffered shipwreck, partly because there was no direct Soviet conflict with Italy during the Ethiopian crisis. As the Italians were busy building Soviet warships throughout this period, it is hardly surprising that the Soviet Union's sanctions on Italy amounted to very little. After that episode, the Russian advocacy of collective security did not cover the hazards of the Soviet Union taking the lead where Britain and France did not.

The Ethiopian disaster and the separation of Italy from France made possible Hitler's occupation of the Rhineland. It frightened the Belgians into neutrality, and it broke the League up completely. The coincidence of the Spanish Civil War – and it was a coincidence – drove Italy further into Germany's arms. Germany and Japan united against Soviet Russia at the same time. The only element left from the various alternative systems which had once seemed open was the British effort to mediate possible areas of dispute with Germany. This policy, however, proved counter-productive. It encouraged rather than deterred Hitler, while focusing his enmity upon Britain.

The first major German advances came in 1938: the Austrian *Anschluss*; then the crisis over Czechoslovakia which threatened a European war at least a year before the British were ready. The September crisis of 1938 provided a clear indication that more was to come, and brought Britain back to her traditional diplomacy – bolstering the Romanian, Turkish and Greek economies against German penetration. Outstanding issues in the Mediterranean were settled with Italy; there was an attempt to concert policy in the Far East with the United States; rearmament was accelerated; and in January 1939 the first tentative attempts were made to repair Anglo-Soviet relations.

The German occupation of Prague on 15 March 1939 led to the final development of British security policy: the attempt to construct a united front with the Balkans and Eastern Europe against what seemed to be the imminent and immediate threat of a new German move. After the Italian action against Albania, which the British Government took to have been concerted with. Germany, the threat of a united Axis policy was seen to have moved into south-east Europe. The Soviets insisted that any joint policy worked out with Britain and France to counter this thrust should centre on a tripartite alliance. The British entered into these negotiations reluctantly and with suspicion – a suspicion which was repaid on the Soviet side. The negotiations came to an end when the Soviets preferred a security conferred by the Nazi offer of a non-aggression pact. This involved the establishment of a common Soviet–German frontier, and recognition of Nazi and Soviet spheres of influence. Russia preferred it to the British offer, which would have put all the onus on the Soviet Union in the event of failure, and from which all the advantages, if it had succeeded, would probably have accrued to the British. Thus the British security policy collapsed, as indeed did all attempts to maintain a common security policy in Europe. The smaller states retreated behind the Declaration of Copenhagen – an illusion of neutrality which (as we have seen) only Sweden and Switzerland were able to maintain once war had begun. Europe in 1939 lacked the confidence and the strength to withstand its own internal pressures. Of these, by far the most important was the creation in Germany of a system of government which denied totally the existence of anything 'European' – or any system at all, save the advancement of Germany to a position of world domination.

It has often been said that the German plans always looked to a war with the Soviet Union, to the expansion of German influence into the Ukraine, and possibly as far as the Urals, thus driving Soviet power back into Asia. But the war which happened in 1939 happened for different reasons. After Munich, German plans turned westwards. The enemy was Britain, not the Soviet Union. In order to secure victory, Hitler had to protect his eastern front. He made very strenuous efforts to come to an agreement with Poland; but his efforts failed completely as a result of misunder-standing and misinterpretations. After the march on Prague (which was only the most preliminary of mopping-up operations, prior to an attack on the west), Hitler was faced with a series of British guarantees. The British guarantee to Poland, and sub-sequently the idea of an Anglo-Polish alliance, turned him against Poland; but the attack on Poland was only a preliminary precaution. The main German attack was still to be against Britain – westwards. If one wants a clue to this, it is found in Hitler's orders of January 1939 which gave priority of allocation of armour plate to the navy. You cannot conquer the Ukraine with battleships. Hitler's primary object was now to drive Britain from the European continent. He had to fulfil an aim which now one finds enshrined on the left wing of British politics. One thing which the British Government had learnt between 1925 and 1939 was that, in terms of security, Britain was a part of Europe and could not be anything else.

We may now conclude with a few reflections about some of the other countries. Italy evinced an irresponsibility personalised in Mussolini. If ever a greater disaster afflicted the Italian race, it would be difficult to recall it. The end of the civil war in Spain led to a retreat into neutrality, which the Spanish were able to maintain until the beginning of the 1970s. A spirit of unrealism and unreality prevailed in Poland, which can only be extenuated because the two alternatives which faced the Poles from a 'realistic' point of view were both totally unacceptable. The Soviet Union and the United States both attempted to retreat into isolation. The French were plagued by uncertainty and division, which was to find its final expression in the vote among the French Generals in September 1939. Out of nineteen or so, only two were in favour of French entry into the war. At the other side of the world, Japan was looking hard for a war in Europe which would free her to pursue her aims in the Far East. She suddenly found that the only way in which that war could come was by Germany concluding a treaty with the country against which the Japanese had been fighting a bitter and entirely losing battle in the innermost parts of Mongolia. Thus the Japanese Government was forced to resign; and Japan and Italy, who had been bought off by British appeasement, were neutrals when war first broke out.

In such conditions, and amid this mass of paradoxes, did the last European war begin.

## NOTES AND REFERENCES

1. Winston S. Churchill, *The Second World War*, 6 vols (London, 1948 *et seq.*, and other editions).
2. 'Cato' (Michael Foot, Frank Owen, P. Howard), *Guilty Men* (London, 1940) is the most famous.
3. A. J. P. Taylor, *The Origins of the Second World War* (London, 1961, and other editions).
4. Martin Gilbert and Richard Gott, *The Appeasers* (London, 1963).
5. Martin Gilbert, *The Roots of Appeasement* (London, 1966).
6. Taylor, *The Origins of the Second World War*, second edn (Harmondsworth, 1964).
7. G.C. Peden, *British Rearmament and the Treasury 1932–1939* (Edinburgh, 1979).
8. J. A. Lukacs, *The Last European War: September 1939–December 1941* (London and Henley, 1976 [1977]).
9. J. M. Keynes (Lord Keynes), *The Economic Consequences of the Peace* (London, 1919, and later editions).

# 2 The German View

## Lothar Kettenacker

Questions which German historians ask about the origins of the Second World War differ to some extent from those which most historians ask in other countries. They differ even more sharply from the questions which Germans themselves used to ask during the interwar period about the origins of the First World War. This second contrast brings out very sharply the change in outlook brought about by unconditional surrender in May 1945. The total collapse of Germany on that occasion exerted a much sharper effect upon subsequent German views and attitudes than did the decision of the German High Command in 1918 to seek an armistice: a decision taken while the army was still entrenched on enemy soil, and the German population was totally unprepared for the sudden turn of events. After the Second World War the Allies learnt their lesson: they abolished the central government and rebuilt Germany from bottom to top. All this they did, however – and this is a crucial point – without concluding a humiliating peace treaty which stipulated categorically Germany's collective guilt for what had happened.[1] Consequently, there was no 'werewolf' organisation[2] defying the occupying powers and assembling 'Hitler cocktails' for World War III, as many people had feared. Nor would nationalist historians emerge at a later date, who would seek to prove Germany's good will before the war.[3] The question was not how the war could have been won or how it could have been averted at the last moment; but rather why nobody managed to stop Hitler from running amok.

Two assumptions were implied in that question. First, it was 'Hitler's War',[4] as *The Times* put it on 2 September 1939, following Chamberlain. Second – and this was an even more doubtful, though less express, proposition – it was implied that Germany's neighbours were as much to blame as the German people who, after all, had been Hitler's first victims in 1933, and who were powerless to influence events thenceforth. During the Cold War, this interpretation served as common ground for a new understanding between Germany and the West, in an attempt to save Europe from the menace of another totalitarian regime. Although a few people like Sir Robert (Lord) Vansittart would argue otherwise,[5] the West had – again in Chamberlain's words – 'no quarrel with the German people except that they allowed themselves to be governed by a Nazi government'.[6] In the meantime, the Nazi system had not only been destroyed by force from the outside, but also the revelations about extermination camps thoroughly discredited it and exposed its utterly criminal character.

Western historians were ready to attribute a fair share of the blame for failure to stop Hitler to their own governments, which had indulged in policies of isolationism and appeasement. While in September 1939 the emphasis on Hitler as the main culprit was a means of psychological warfare designed to stave off the 'bloody war' by a revolt in Germany,[7] his place in the dock after 1945 permitted the Germans to repress further investigations into their own past. There was, in the 1950s and early 1960s, some kind of tacit understanding that Western historiography was to examine the approach of war in the international context, whereas it was the job of the German historian to explain the downfall of Weimar and Hitler's rise to the top inside Germany.[8]

By common consent, the economic depression figured very prominently in the destruction of the Weimar republic. It discredited the democratic system, which had been adopted in 1918–19 partly for the sake of better peace terms, but which now proved itself incapable of preventing mass unemployment and thus led to a further polarisation of German society. The spectacular success of the Nazi Party in the elections of 1930 seemed to prove without doubt that the great depression was the crucial turning point. Once Hitler had seized power, given his social-Darwinist belief in the German need for *Lebensraum*, war was inevitable. The timing was just a matter of how Hitler could manipulate international relations to carry out his so-called *Programm* or *Stufenplan*.

That view is not altogether mistaken, but it is somewhat simplistic. It was first seriously challenged by two books published in the early 1960s – or rather by the unforeseen repercussions of those books. Fritz Fischer's *Griff nach der Weltmacht*[9] showed to his generation of historians that Imperial Germany did precipitate the outbreak of the First World War – after they had striven to prove the opposite and thought the issue settled once and for all. By exposing Germany's very ambitious war aims during the Great War, Fischer provided some of the missing links between the Second and the Third Reich, between the plans of the German High Command under Ludendorff and Hindenburg, and Hitler's vision of a German Ukraine. Fischer has since reaffirmed his thesis by stressing the continuing alliance of the traditional élites in the Foreign Office with those in industry and in the army.[10]

In many ways A. J. P. Taylor's study on the origins of the Second World War[11] made the same points. This book was greatly misunderstood in Germany, as German academics are not accustomed to provocative historiography which is intended to be stimulating rather than reliable in every detail. Taylor tried to build the bridge from the other side by cutting Hitler down to size, and placing him firmly within the tradition of German revisionism. German historians were incensed by the way Taylor interpreted available evidence, attempting to show that Hitler was no more than a ruthless opportunist carried along in the pursuit of revisionist policies, until he overstepped the mark on 1 September 1939. His views were, incidentally, very close to those of the British Government at the time, who were so absorbed by the cleverness of Hitler's techniques which led him from one bloodless victory to another that they overlooked the ideological streak in his long-term plans.[12] However, what might be disastrous in the conduct of foreign policy – a confusion over rational tactics and dogmatic aims – can be very illuminating in historiographical terms. Taylor did not attempt to exculpate the German dictator, but to shift the responsibilities from Hitler's shoulders to the shoulders of those who had supported him at home, and of those who had tried to appease him abroad.

However, it took German historians quite some time to realise something which was all too evident for other historians, namely that though Hitler might have started the war, it was the German army, led by a predominantly Prussian officer corps, which attacked Poland and not an assortment of SA- or SS-battalions. In the course of this discovery, the whole of German history was subjected to a thorough reinvestigation and reassessment. The previous dogma that German history was dominated not by domestic factors but by foreign policy considerations was turned upside down.[13] However, it appeared to be much easier to trace the domestic influences on the conduct of foreign policy in Bismarckian or Wilhelmine Germany than in the Third Reich. Hitler himself turned out to be the stumbling block for the *'Primat der Innenpolitik'*, because both the importance of foreign policy in Nazi Germany and the impact of Hitler's own decisions are indisputable. Theories on Fascism do not furnish an answer to the problem of why the Germans followed Hitler into the war with so little enthusiasm,[14] despite a barrage of militaristic propaganda. Abstract models are always a distortion of history because they do not allow for contradictions.

One of the main features of the Nazi system was its ambivalence.[15] It was both conservative and revolutionary, both ideologically motivated and nihilistic. From the outside it appeared to be well organised, yet at the same time it was a madhouse of chaotic and competing power structures.[16] One is bound to be misled if one focuses on one aspect at the expense of others. The inherent contradictions in the system have a tendency to confuse historians as much as they fooled the German conservatives and foreign statesmen in the 1930s: men who, in their search for a clear-cut analysis, underestimated Hitler and the nature of his regime by seeing them only in their own terms of reference.[17] Hitler's success was due, to a large extent, to the fact that he was constantly misjudged by his enemies: by the left he was seen as a mere tool in the hands of capitalism, by the conservatives as an inexperienced, incompetent demagogue with a mass following. By foreign statesmen in the 1930s he was seen as a Machiavellian revisionist who tried to annul the results of the Versailles treaty.

Historians' views, at least in Germany, are very often determined by the topic of their first research project, and this leads them to exaggerate the relevance of their findings. For some time now the debate has been shaped by the controversy between the 'intentionalist' and 'functionalist' schools, to use the terminology of the Oxford historian Tim Mason.[18] The most outspoken representative of the latter, Hans Mommsen, who has done some excellent research into the German civil service under the Nazi system, has come to the conclusion that in many ways Hitler was a weak dictator whose incompetent handling of the government machine led to a process of what he calls 'cumulative radicalisation', brought about by one emergency situation after another.[19] Tim Mason has since applied this thesis to the outbreak of war in 1939, which he depicts as the result of an overheated economy preparing for war and eventually banking on it.[20] Yet one should not overlook the fact that Hitler used such crises for his own ends. Moreover, the British Government, for the sake of a general settlement, was only too anxious to help Germany out of any economic crisis as is shown by the secret negotiations of Göring's envoy in London in the summer of 1939.[21]

On the other hand, Klaus Hildebrand, who has written the only concise history of Nazi foreign policy,[22] strongly believes that the war was caused by Hitler's *Programm*, dogmatic in its aims and calculated in its execution. Together with Andreas Hillgruber, he maintains that the regime must be judged by its worst crimes, the pitiless war in the East and the 'final solution', not by its internal power structures which it shared to some extent with other fascist regimes.[23] Hildebrand admits, however, that the partial identity of interests between Hitler and the conservative élites is crucial for the initial efficiency of the regime.

If a synthesis of these two approaches is to be achieved, more weight must be given to the degree of support for the regime afforded by the traditional élites and by the German people at large. Hitler did not move in a political vacuum.[24] After 1933 he applied the same tactics in foreign policy as he had used during his struggle to the centre of power. The seizure of power in 1933 was not a goal in itself but a stepping stone towards the systematic realisation of a vast empire in the East of 'Aryan' race, the utopia of a mad artist who had turned to politics. To achieve these ambitions, Hitler required the collaboration of the traditional experts in diplomacy, industry, the civil service, and particularly in the army. As a product of the Imperial Army, Hitler felt much more respect for the officer corps of the Prussian army than for his own SA. In aligning himself with the conservative élites rather than relying on his *'alte Kämpfer'* he consolidated his power and gained respect abroad. Hitler was not interested in social re-volution, or nationalisation of the means of production, or an exchange of élites; but he skilfully employed the threat of a second revolution to secure support, and to undermine and even-tually corrupt the existing social fabric.

The common platform of this unholy alliance was the fight

against the constraints of Versailles. The conservative élites went along, as did the rest of the German people, with Hitler's systematic abolition of Versailles without ever defining the limitation of the policy upon which their collaboration rested. Under Hitler's rule and the influence of the *Volksgemeinschafts-propaganda* Germany experienced a fragmentation of her political power structures which were all left to develop their own dynamics. This was particularly true of industry, which bene-fited from the rearmament programme, and of the *Reichswehr* which was not swamped by the SA and yet was greatly enlarged by the introduction of military service in 1935. Once the parties, trade unions and other political forces were destroyed, there was no remaining power centre outside the army with any chance of effective resistance to Hitler's plans. What impressed army leaders most was the concept of a more or less totally militarised society, particularly the paramilitary training of the young generation, which had been neglected by the democratic parties.[25] From 1927 onwards, schemes for a regimentation of society seemed to have gained wide circulation. The moment democracy weakened, the experiences of the war were held up as a model for a better and more efficiently run society.[26] Under General von Schleicher, Hitler's predecessor, the army tried un-successfully to win the trade unions over and to gain the necessary mass support which it so badly needed for both political and professional ends: for overcoming the economic crisis through rearmament, in violation of the Versailles treaty, and for a popular militia organisation which would be capable of sup-plementing the *Reichswehr*, hitherto confined to 100 000 men. A society organised and educated along regimental lines corresponded to the idea of a corporative state which had so much appeal to conservatives and National Socialists alike. It seemed to be the ideal solution in an increasingly class-ridden and polarised society.

In the circumstances, it appears to me, a military dictatorship under General von Schleicher was the only alternative to Hitler. It would have been less popular, but more open to gradual and controlled change. By the end of 1932 there was no hope of saving democracy – it had already broken down – and the only question was what was to follow. Today we know that a military dictator-ship, detestable as it is, would probably have been a hundred times better than letting Hitler have a go – the 'Bohemian Lance

Corporal', as President Hindenburg called him. However, apart from the fact that it was asking the impossible to have a govern-ment of the right, let alone the extreme right, with the support of the trade unions, yet it was not clear to contemporaries why a military dictatorship should have been preferable to Hitler. He was much more popular than the Junker generals, and in this sense more democratic, and in Germany there has always been a certain inclination towards a somewhat dogmatic understanding of democracy – in the French sense of *'volontée générale'*.

In many ways, the generals thought that Hitler was their puppet, the public relations agent who would allow them to get on with their job of moulding the army into a more suitable instrument for power-politics. On 3 February, General von Blomberg, the new Minister of Defence, described Hitler's appointment a few days before as 'the realisation of what many of the best had aspired to' and had regarded as the 'most appropriate precondition for the military training and education of the whole population'.[27] In the following years the identity of interests between Hitler and the armed forces went very far indeed: Hitler initiated a very ambitious rearmament programme in defiance of the Versailles treaty, introduced military service in 1935 and occupied the demilitarised Rhineland a year later. For the officer corps this meant an opening up of new careers and increased prestige at home and abroad. A strong army was seen as a means of backing up foreign policy and of negotiating from a position of strength. The generals did not object in principle to the idea of a limited war for limited gains, if political manoeuvres failed. War was not immoral; it might just be too risky.

If the General Staff prepared for war, as most General Staffs do, it was for professional reasons: to be ready for war if necessary. It was not because they had deliberately and con-sciously embarked on a course for war. Here a certain amount of confusion arose, since preparing for war for the purpose of actually waging it was exactly what Hitler had in mind when he revealed his future plans and calculations to the German High Command. He was no longer just another politician or a military expert, but someone who was deadly serious and meant what he said. He saw himself as another and more successful Bismarck who would choose his political terrain carefully for a succession of quick and decisive blows. He hoped thereby to create a vast new empire almost overnight before anyone woke up, similar to

Bismarck's achievement in 1870/71. Whereas he knew what he wanted, the generals did not; but they were favourably disposed towards his approach. They faced every crisis which Hitler provoked with trepidation, knowing full well that Germany was not prepared for a showdown. Then they concurred with him after the successful outcome, as did the rest of their countrymen. Hitherto the Prussian generals have been criticised by historians for being too ambitious and too influential in political matters. It seems more appropriate to assume the opposite. They were only too keen to abdicate from their political responsibilities[28] (which they were bound to have in any dictatorship, whether they liked it or not), concentrating on their *Kriegshandwerk*, as the German historian Ritter[29] called it, and leaving *Staatskunst* to Hitler, who did indeed regard himself as a *Künstler* in matters of politics.

The emasculation of the generals was formalised after Hindenberg's death. Hitler assumed supreme command of the armed forces, demanding the oath of loyalty from every soldier to the 'Führer and Reichskanzler Adolf Hitler'. Ever since, the German generals have shielded behind this ceremonial and pseudo-legal abdication of responsibility. If one wants to understand the process by which the army was drawn into the war, it is of crucial important to grasp the impact of Hitler's breathtaking successes in foreign policy which coincided so well with long-established national aspirations and strategic goals. Why, they asked themselves, should Hitler precipitate a two-front war if he proved to be a master of bloodless victories? He persuaded the generals that by handling war with the same skilful hand as diplomacy he could solve all of Germany's imaginary problems. Nothing was impossible if they backed him in his policy of calculated risks; but risks had to be taken. The German General Staff was not averse to refighting the First World War under more propitious circumstances and a more inspiring leadership – possibly as a succession of short sharp wars rather than long campaigns – if this was the only avenue to establishing Germany's role as a world power, on an equal footing with the British Empire and the United States of America. It is open to argument whether this course would not also have led to war – either with Hitler or some more traditionally minded general at the helm. Still, it would have saved the world from the holocaust of systematic genocide against Jews and Russians. It is hard to see how France and Soviet Russia could have been persuaded to become German satellites without the use of force. Establishing German overlordship over Europe, as in the Middle Ages, could not just follow the pattern of German unification under Prussia by an even more ruthless Iron Chancellor. Again the difference must be stressed as much as the striking parallels: war remained the *ultima ratio* of politics in line with traditional objectives; it was not to be precipitated at the earliest moment, at the greatest risk, and for immeasurable gains.

Yet Hitler was pressed for time. In 1933 he ordered the army to be ready for a *Blitzkrieg* strategy by 1939; in 1937 he decided that the question of German living space must be tackled by 1942–3 at the latest. This foreshadowed the war in the East – Hitler's truly 'final solution'. There were two reasons why Hitler was so anxious to get on with this timetable: one rational, the other irrational. The 'irrational reason' was that something might happen to him – the only genius in German history capable of achieving the great breakthrough – and then the momentum would be lost. The 'rational reason' was that Germany was bound to be overtaken in a general rearmament race by her enemies – notably by Great Britain – unless she enlarged her economic resources by conquest or by subjection of neighbouring countries. In other words, when it eventually dawned upon Western statesmen what Germany was up to, time was already running out for Hitler's plans. In about 1937, Hitler realised that Great Britain – or 'England', as he preferred to call it – might allow him to consolidate the German nation-state, but not more. Britain would certainly not allow him to establish a position of clear hegemony in Europe.[30] He would not be drawn when, in November 1937, Halifax indicated that the British Government was prepared to make concessions with regard to Austria, the Sudeten area, Danzig and the Corridor – and possibly even the question of the German colonies – provided that peace was preserved.

Here one might pause for a moment to consider Hitler's attitude towards Great Britain, a country which proved to be more obstinate than he had allowed for in his original plans or 'programme'. There is a certain inclination among British historians to assume that, since Hitler was Britain's Enemy Number One, so also must Britain have occupied the corresponding position in Hitler's mind. Hitler greatly admired the British Empire, about which he knew next to nothing, and the British upper class which figured as his model of a master race. Indeed, his great hero was Cecil Rhodes who was known to have favoured an alliance with Germany. When he formed his ideas about an alliance with Britain, notably in his so-called 'Second Book', around 1928,[31] he imagined that the ruling élite had remained as imperialist in outlook as in the nineteenth century.[32] He persuaded himself that Great Britain was no longer interested in a strictly European balance of power – provided no European power challenged her maritime supremacy, as the incompetent Kaiser had done before 1914. There was no ground for antagonism provided each side respected each other's sphere of interest. The Anglo-German Naval Agreement of 18 June 1935 was supposed to have been Hitler's 'happiest day'.[33] He reasoned that if Germany refrained from rebuilding a powerful navy and showed no interest in regaining control over her former colonies, Britain would not make a fuss about Germany's drive for a continental empire. But a fuss she was to make from now on, each time Hitler further consolidated Germany's power base in Europe. The big question was whether Britain would stand idle and limit her response to diplomatic disapproval when the Reich was ready for the great trek to the East, the resumption of the *'Germanenzug nach Osten'*, in search of new living space.

Clearly, Britain's role always remained subordinate to Hitler's territorial aims in Eastern Europe. Josef Henke has analysed his changing attitudes very aptly by stressing that he first based his plans on an alliance *with* Britain, then moved on to the idea of taking action *without* her but not *against* her if this could be avoided – only to end up doing just that.[34] From the point of view of Hitler's *Programm* the Munich conference had a very different meaning from that which it took for the rest of the world at the time, or for historians today: it was neither a colossal triumph for Germany nor the climax of appeasement, but a failure; because the German dictator would have preferred to occupy the whole of Bohemia and Moravia rather than accept a settlement along ethnic lines at the hands of the Western Allies. Munich pointed to Britain's continued interest in Europe and clearly showed how far she was prepared to go: a general settlement of all Germany's rightful grievances, but no more. Hence Hitler's intense propaganda campaign was directed against Britain soon after Munich, against the trespassing *Gouvernante* (governess), teaching morals instead of minding her own business (which was not beyond reproach).[35] While this sort of denunciation of Britain's peace-keeping role was meant to prepare the German people for war, for an 'enforced war', the result was a hardening of public opinion in Britain against appeasement. And while Hitler tried to force Britain out of Europe, the British Government, though inclined to grant a certain amount of regional preponderance to Germany, reluctantly involved herself in Europe more than ever before.

The fact that Hitler was not to be appeased has preoccupied historians so much that they have ignored the question, whether he could have been deterred if Britain had adopted some radically different policy immediately after Munich. Suppose, for example, that Britain had dramatically adjusted her overall policy to the mind of an unpredictable continental dictator: by taking Churchill into the Government, setting up a Ministry of Supply, introducing conscription and building up an impressive bomber force, to the complete disregard of her economic resources. Would all of this have made any difference? Unless one can unhesitatingly answer such questions in the affirmative, one should be cautious about condemning Chamberlain out of hand.[36] One thing which Chamberlain never even considered giving was the one concession Hitler wanted from Britain: a *carte blanche* for German *Blitzkrieg* imperialism in Eastern Europe.

The British guarantee to Warsaw was an unforeseen roadblock to Hitler. It meant that Poland could not be drawn into concluding some dubious alliance with Germany, but had to be 'finished off'. While the world was focusing on Danzig, and wondering whether it was worth dying to prevent the incorporation of this ethnically German city into the Reich, from Hitler's point of view the whole question of Danzig and the conquest of Poland was only the gateway to further expansion eastwards. Shortly after Britain had guaranteed Polish independence[37] – not Poland's territorial integrity, it should be noted – in a last desperate effort to stop Hilter, he ordered the *Wehrmacht* to be ready for attack by 1 September (*Fall Weiß*, 3 April 1939).

Poland served as the ideal bait for conservative German élites, especially for the aristocratic officer corps, with its strong foothold in the eastern provinces. A short, lightning campaign against the Poles which would reconnect East Prussia with the Reich was to the liking of many estate owners. It was in many ways a more popular enterprise than the annexation of Czechoslovakia which could only be justified for strategic reasons: a much shortened frontier, the intake of the Sudeten Germans to the army and a welcome arsenal of weapons. Furthermore, Poland had always been the common ground for an alliance between Russia and Prussia. Russians and Germans would always agree to keep her weak and dismembered. It was not only Ribbentrop's anti-British diplomacy[38] that made the non-aggression treaty with Moscow possible. The contribution of Graf Friedrich Werner von der Schulenberg, the German ambassador who later joined the plot of 20 July, must not be underrated either. Research into the business connections of German industrialists with the Soviet Union[39] suggests that a treaty with the ideological arch enemy, an understanding between two forms of National Socialism, was welcomed in unexpected quarters. The keen interest in improving relations with Russia shown by the aristocratic and industrial élites was very misleading as far as the scrutinising of German intentions by Western diplomats was concerned. Contacts with German conservatives who tended to look down on the Nazi leadership were much more easily established than with Hitler and his entourage. The intelligence gained from such social occasions as hunting with the *Reichsmarschall*, so greatly cherished by Nevile Henderson,[40] the British Ambassador, was not very reliable, to say the least. The conservative élite tended to be conceited about their political influence and too rational about Germany's resources and requirements to be truly representative of the utopian and racialist hard core of the regime headed by Hitler.

Conversations with such German diplomats and businessmen suggested that Germany was striving for an 'informal' empire in the East, brought about by economic penetration and the force of Greater Germany's natural weight: that the nonsensical *Lebensraum* ideology could be discounted. For British appeasers, this would seem the most sensible course for Germany to take, the most rewarding of all bloodless victories.[41] It was one of those attractive illusions which recommend themselves by their common sense. It had the same kind of appeal to the West as Hitler's claim that he wished for nothing else but to accommodate all ethnic Germans under one roof. The seizure of Prague demonstrated beyond doubt that the slogan of self-determination was only a propaganda weapon which served to legitimise immediate demands and disguise future ambitions. It cast great doubt on whether Hitler had the same ideas as Hjalmar Schacht when he demanded a 'free hand' in the East. When he relieved Schacht of his post as President of the *Reichsbank*,[42] and went on to turn Bohemia and Moravia into a German *Protekιorat*, there was every reason to doubt the peaceful nature of Hitler's eastward expansion. As we know, and should have known at the time, for the German dictator a 'free hand' meant one that was not clothed in a 'kid glove', as he later put it in his table talks during the was.[43] After all resistance had been destroyed, the East was to be the 'Far West' for the settlers from Swabia and other German *Gaue*, with Himmler's SS cast as the United States cavalry, making use (to quote Hitler's table talks once again) of four-metre rail tracks and *Autobahnen* eleven metres wide.[44]

Whether Hitler could have been deterred from attempting to realise these fantasies if he had failed to reach a provisional settlement with Moscow is a matter for speculation. It seems certain, however, that Britain's pact with an indefensible ally such as Poland never offered any prospect of stopping him. All frantic efforts by the British Government towards the end of August to bring Germany and Poland to the conference table were foredoomed to failure. Berlin had already designed a scenario for breaking up the conference in the event that a Polish plenipotentiary arrived in time.[45] Hitler dreaded a second Munich as much as Warsaw and London did: it could not possibly yield more than Danzig and a stretch of territory linking it with the Reich. Something more dramatic was called for than Chamberlain's carefully phrased warning about the imminence of war: a convincing show of strength and resolution by all major powers, including the United States and the Soviet Union, which would have driven home to German élites in the army and industry that Hitler had pushed the country to the brink of disaster. Sometimes one wonders whether a Hollywood film director with an acute sense of the spectacular might not have been a better advisor to the British Government than, say, Sir Alexander Cadogan of the Foreign Office.

The question of *how* it all happened – Hitler's seizure of power, the drive towards war and holocaust – can be answered with more assurance of credibility than the fundamental question: *why* did it happen, how was it possible for so many decent people to be induced to follow a 'madman'[45] into world war and misery of unprecedented magnitude? Historians tend to think that telling the story, or rather analysing the decisions taken at every point along the way is, after all, the best possible answer to any further probing. This method, however suitable for historical problems in general, has never satisfied those who need definite answers to put their minds at rest in view of the sheer monstrosity of the Nazi record. This search for a definite explanation, and the lessons to be drawn from the comparatively recent past by present-day politics, have led to a variety of theories on Fascism.[47] The Marxist interpretation tries to monopolise our understanding by singling out the 'crisis of capitalism', the liberal interpretation stresses the totalitarian character of the regime, the socio-psychological interpretation selects its repressive and authoritarian stand, the socio-logical interpretation points out the problems of modernisation. Ernst Nolte has seen Fascism as an ideology transcending politics, while others have alluded to the continuity of German history from 'Luther to Hitler'.

All such theories exaggerate certain aspects of 'Fascism' to the exclusion of others, and distort history for the benefit of a more discursive historiography – which appears to be the requirement of students and teachers of history. Taken as a whole, they add up to a comprehensive picture of the most decisive forces and features which moulded the face of this epoch. Yet these theories should be rejected because of the monocausal approach and dogmatic rigour inherent in most of them. It is already very doubtful and indeed controversial whether it makes sense to talk indiscriminately of 'Fascism', which was, in the first instance, an Italian phenomenon. It was Hitler's, and not Mussolini's, utopian racialism and territorial Darwinism which changed the course of world history and gave Fascism such an incomparably bad name. There is much to be said for using the contemporary term *Hitler-Bewegung* when referring to National Socialism before 1933, and calling the disastrous twelve years which were to follow the *Drittes Reich*.

This is perhaps the best way to stress the historical authenticity of the 'German Dictatorship',[48] which is in danger of being swamped by political prejudice. Most of the theories would not dispute that the social basis of National Socialism was the middle class, more specifically the greatly expanded and politically volatile lower *'Mittelstand'* of Weimar Germany, which amounted to well over 40 per cent of German society in 1933 and of whom nearly one million were out of work.[49] The so-called 'old'

and 'new' *Mittelstand* provided the enthusiastic mass following
which brought Hitler to power – or at least to the threshold of
power, before he was let in by the conservative élites – and
furnished the unswerving loyalty which enabled him to embark on
his policy of challenging the whole civilised world. Hitler became
the charismatic overlord of this stratum of society: small artisans,
shopkeepers, farmers (*alter Mittelstand*) and petty civil servants,
clerks and to some extent foremen (*neuer Mittelstand*). They
looked upon themselves as the most hard-working, decent and
deserving, yet badly neglected, section of society. It is not appropriate to describe them as 'middle class' or 'bourgeois'; rather they
were represented by the ordinary German *Bürger*, the 'man in the
pub' who expected everybody to conform to his own standards of
*Anstand* (propriety). Their identification with the nation and her
fortunes was complete: they were shocked by the sudden, unexpected defeat in 1918, were disgusted by the revolutionary
turmoil which followed, resented the new men at the top who
lacked 'dignity', that is, did not satisfy the popular desire for a
display of imperial grandeur, felt alienated by the spread of
anonymous bureaucracies, rejected Berlin fashion and avant-
garde culture as *undeutsch*, loathed Jewish entrepreneurs and
their upper-class lifestyle, dismissed all left-wing intellectuals as
being Communist agitators, suffered the effects of the 1923
inflation which destroyed their modest savings and blamed the
economic crisis of 1929 (which led to a slump in food prices,
salary cuts and large-scale bankruptcy in small businesses) on the
impotence of parliamentary democracy. Their man was Hitler
who promised a dramatic change of direction without going into
details and revealing his more sinister plans.

To call these people 'fascist' or their approval of Hitler's regime
something like 'affirmative integration'[50] is rather meaningless:
they deserve all the attention, if not sympathy, of the middle-class
historian who has hitherto been inclined either to ignore them or
to dismiss them for their lack of political awareness or class con-
sciousness. They most certainly did not vote for war and genocide
but they were not sufficiently anti-militarist and anti-racialist in
outlook to demonstrate against the Nuremberg laws before the
hostile eyes of the police, or to refuse obedience when military
duty called. They could easily be persuaded that the *Führer* was
the true *paterfamilias* who knew what was best for Germany, for
the German *Volksgemeinschaft* which embraced all classes (or

rather *Stände*, that is, trades and professions), denominations and regions of the greater Fatherland. By 1938 his record did indeed look impressive: he had united Germany as never before, both internally and externally, led Germany out of the economic depression, wiped out the 'shame of Versailles' by lifting all restrictions on Germany imposed by her former enemies, staged the most rewarding Olympic Games, initiated all kinds of new ventures to overcome social divisions and to bridge geographical distances, and shown equal kindness to young and old, poor and rich, on his numerous trips around the country: sitting next to the driver in an open motor car, visibly unpretentious in his personal manners. Why on earth should this super star turn out to be the political archcriminal of the modern world?

## NOTES AND REFERENCES

1. This sort of peace was already recommended as early as 1942 by the historian and journalist E. H. Carr who had been with the Foreign Office at one time. See his book, *Conditions of Peace* (London, 1942).
2. As to the propaganda aspect see now Michael Balfour, *Propaganda in War, 1939–45* (London, 1979) pp. 406–10.
3. Strangely enough the only apologetic historians in that matter are not from Germany but from Britain – David Irving, *Hitler's War* (New York, 1977); and from the United States – David L. Hoggan, Der erzwungene Krieg (Tübingen, 1961).
4. Franklin R. Gannon, *The British Press and Germany* (Oxford, 1971) pp. 284–7.
5. Robert G. Vansittart, *Black Record: Germans Past and Present* (London, 1941).
6. *Parliamentary Debates, House of Commons*, vol. 351, col. 131 (1 September 1939).
7. Cf. Maurice Cowling, *The Impact of Hitler* (Chicago, 1977) p. 12.
8. The most important contribution at that time was the work by Karl Dietrich Bracher, Wolfgang Sauer and Gerhard Schulz, *Die Nationalsozialistische Machtergreifung: Studien zur Errichtung des totalitären Herrschaftssystems in Deutschland 1933/1934* (Köln, 1962).
9. Fritz Fischer, *Griff nach der Weltmacht* (Düsseldorf, 1964). See also his subsequent study, *Der Krieg der Illusionen* (Düsseldorf, 1969).
10. Fritz Fischer, *Bündnis der Eliten* (Düsseldorf, 1979).
11. A. J. P. Taylor, *The Origins of the Second World War*, (Harmondsworth, 1964). See also Taylor, *1939 Revisited*, the 1981 Annual Lecture of the German Historical Institute, London.
12. See Lothar Kettenacker, 'Die Diplomatie der Ohnmacht' in *Sommer 1939*, ed. Wolfgang Benz and Hermann Graml (Stuttgart, 1979) pp. 223–79. This

impression is also evident in Sidney Aster, *1939: the Making of the Second World War* (London, 1973).

13. It must be said, however, that most historians who attempted to prove this thesis concentrated on the period before 1914, notably Hans Ulrich Wehler, *Bismarck und der Imperialismus* (Köln/Berlin, 1972) and Volker R. Berghahn, *Der Tirpitz-Plan* (Düsseldorf, 1971).

14. Cf. Balfour, *Propaganda in War*, pp. 148–51, and Marlis G. Steinert, *Hitler's War and the Germans: Public Mood and Attitude during the Second World War*, translated from German (Athens: Ohio University Press, 1977).

15. See Karl Dietrich Bracher, 'Tradition and Revolution im Nationalsozialismus' in *Hitler, Deutschland und die Mächte*, ed. Manfred Funke (Düsseldorf, paperback, 1978) pp. 17–29.

16. See the standard work by Martin Broszat, 'Der Staat Hitlers' in *Deutsche Geschichte seit dem Ersten Weltkrieg*, vol. I (Stuttgart, 1971) pp. 501–839; also Peter Diehl-Thiele, *Partei und Staat im Dritten Reich* (München, 1969) and in English the collection of essays in P. D. Stachura (ed.), *The Shaping of the Nazi State* (London, 1978).

17. See Philipp W. Fabry, *Mutmaßungen über Hitler: Urteile von Zeitgenossen* (Düsseldorf, 1969) – on Britain: pp. 199–222.

18. Tim Mason, 'Intention and Explanation: a Current Controversy about the Interpretation of National Socialism' in G. Hirschfeld and L. Kettenacker (eds), *The 'Führer State': Myth and Reality* (Stuttgart, 1981) pp. 23–42.

19. Hans Mommsen, 'Ausnahmezustand als Herrschaftstechnik des NS-Regimes' in Funke (ed.) *Hitler, Deutschland und die Mächte*, pp. 30–45. See also his article, 'Hitlers Stellung im nationalsozialistischen Herrschaftssystem' in Hirschfeld and Kettenacker (eds), *The 'Führer State'*.

20. Tim Mason, 'Zur Funktion des Angriffskriegs 1939' in Gilbert Ziebura (ed.) *Grundfragen deutscher Außenpolitik seit 1871* (Darmstadt, 1975) pp. 376–416. Mason has since qualified his conclusions somewhat by stressing that this is *not* to argue that Hitler was forced to go to war in the sense of not wanting to. Cf. his article, 'Intention and Explanation'.

21. Bernd Jörgen Wendt, *Economic Appeasement: Handel und Finanzen in der britischen Deutschlandpolitik 1933–1939* (Düsseldorf, 1971) pp. 606–8.

22. Klaus Hildebrand, *Deutsche Außenpolitik 1933–1945: Kalkül oder Dogma?*, 3rd edn (Stuttgart, 1976).

23. Klaus Hildebrand, *Das Dritte Reich* (München, 1979) pp. 86–8. Andreas Hillgruber, 'Die "Endlösung" und das deutsche Ostimperium als Kernstück des rassenideologischen Programms des Nationalsozialismus' in *Deutsche Großmacht- und Weltpolitik im 19 und 20 Jahrhundert* (Düsseldorf, 1977) pp. 252–75.

24. See the excellent intermediate chapters, 'Zwischenbetrachtungen' in Joachim C. Fest's biography *Hitler* (Frankfurt/Main and Berlin, 1973).

25. Wolfram Wette, 'Ideologie, Propaganda and Innenpolitik als Voraussetzungen der Kriegspolitik des Dritten Reiches' in *Das Deutsche Reich und der Zweite Weltkrieg*, vol. I: *Ursachen und Voraussetzungen der Deutschen Kriegspolitik*, ed. by Wilhelm Deist, Manfred Messerschmidt and others (Stuttgart, 1979) pp. 121–8. This should now be seen as the indispensable standard work on Germany's preparation for the Second World War.

26. Hans-Erich Volkmann, 'Die NS-Wirtschaft in Vorbereitung des Krieges', ibid., pp. 177–89.
27. Quoted in Wette, 'Ideologie, Propaganda and Innenpolitik', p. 122.
28. See Wilhelm Deist, 'Die Aufrüstung der Wehrmacht' in Deist *et al.*, *Das Deutsche Reich und der Zweite Weltkrieg*, vol. I, p. 532.
29. Gerhard Ritter, *Staatskunst and Kriegshandwerk*, 4 vols (München, 1954–1968). This is the most comprehensive study on the problem of militarism in German history between 1740 and 1918.
30. Cf. Hildebrand, *Deutsche Außenpolitik*, pp. 55–63; also Josef Henke, *England in Hitlers politischem Kalkül 1935–1939* (Boppard, 1973) pp. 109–86.
31. *Hitlers Zweites Buch*, ed. by Gerhard L. Weinberg (Stuttgart, 1961) pp. 164–75.
32. Henry Picker (ed.), *Hitlers Tischgespräche im Führerhauptquartier* (Stuttgart, 1976) p. 224 (18 April 1942).
33. Robert Ingrim, *Hitlers Glücklichster Tag* (Stuttgart, 1962); see also Jost Dülffer, *Weimar, Hitler und die Marine: Reichspolitik und Flottenbau 1920–1939* (Düsseldorf, 1973).
34. Josef Henke, 'Hitlers England-Konzeption: Formulierung und Realisierungsversuche' in Funke (ed.), *Hitler, Deutschland und die Mächte*, p. 594.
35. Cf. his speech in Saarbrücken on 9 October 1938, in Max Domarus (ed.), *Hitler: Reden und Proklamationen*, vol. I (München, 1965) p. 956. See also Henke, *England in Hitlers politischem Kalkül*, pp. 187–204.
36. As to the problem of appeasement see Anthony P. Adamwhaite, *The Making of the Second World War* (London 1979) pp. 61–75 and the literature he lists on p. 231.
37. See Simon Newman, *March 1939: The British Guarantee to Poland* (Oxford, 1976).
38. Wolfgang Michalka, *Ribbentrop und die deutsche Weltpolitik, 1933–1940* (München, 1980); reviewed in the *Bulletin* of the German Historical Institute, 6, 1981, pp. 14–17. See also his article, 'Conflicts within the German Leadership on the Objectives and Tactics of German Foreign Policy 1933–1939' in L. Kettenacker and W. J. Mommsen (eds), *The Fascist Challenge and the Policy of Appeasement* (London, forthcoming).
39. Cf. Hartmut Pogge von Strandmann, 'Großindustrie und Rapallopolitik: Deutsch–sowjetische Handesbeziehungen in der Weimarer Republik' in *Historische Zeitschrift*, vol. 222, 1976, pp. 265–341.
40. See his memoirs, *Failure of a Mission* (London, 1940).
41. Cf. David Dilks (ed.), *The Diaries of Sir Alexander Cadogan* (London, 1971) p. 116–20.
42. See Wendt, *Economic Appeasement* p. 535 on the British reaction to Schacht's dismissal.
43. Hitler urged his men during the war to take the Teutonic Knights as a shining example who had not won the East with 'Glacéhandschuhen' but with the bible and the sword. Picker, *Hitlers Tischgespräche*, p. 285 (12 December 1942).
44. Ibid., p. 247 (27 April 1942) and p. 440 (18 July 1942).
45. Diary of the Chief of the General Staff, Franz Halder, *Kriegstagebuch*, vol. I (Stuttgart, 1962) p. 42.

46. Chamberlain called him 'the accursed madman' (Cowling, *The Impact of Hilter*, p. 356).

47. Among the many surveys the most comprehensive and detached are: Wolfgang Wippermann, *Faschismustheorien* (Darmstadt, 1976); Richard Saage, *Faschismustheorien* (München, 1976); Renzo De Felice, *Interpretations of Fascism* (Cambridge, Mass, 1977).

48. Programmatic title of Karl Dietrich Bracher's analysis of National Socialism, *Die Deutsche Diktatur* (Köln, 1969).

49. *Statistisches Jahrbuch für das Deutsche Reich*, 53. Jg. (Berlin, 1934) p. 19. Civil Servants and employees, 17.1%; Family employees ('mithelfende Familienangehörige' i.e. of farmers, small shopkeepers, etc.), 16.4%; self-employed (including farmers, etc.), 16.4%. At least half of the latter category can be regarded as lower middle class. See also Broszat, 'Der Staat Hitlers', pp. 530–42, who emphasises that the NSDAP was particularly attractive to young people (70% of members joining between 1930 and 1933 were under 40, 43% between 18 and 30 years old).

50. A term which has cropped up in discussions at a conference organised by the German Historical Institute in 1979. See Introduction by W. J. Mommsen to *The 'Führer State'*, ed. Hirschfeld and Kettenacker. As to the ensuing controversy arising from this conference see Klaus Hildebrand, 'Nationalsozialismus ohne Hitler' in *Geschichte in Wissenschaft und Unterricht (GWU) 1980/5*, pp. 289–304; Karl Heinz Bohrer, 'Hitler oder die Deutschen' in *Frankfurter Allgemeine Zeitung*, 25 May 1979; and W. J. Mommsen's reply in *GWU*.

# 3 The British View

## A. J. P. Taylor

I am able to take a very detached view about the outbreak of the Polish war, because I spent the whole summer of 1939 in Savoy, and only returned to England the day after the war started. Thus I am little influenced by contemporary impressions. My own impression in Savoy was quite simple – it was enshrined in a simple judgement: 'These people won't fight'. Although it looked as if I was wrong when the war broke out, it turned out soon that I was quite right.

There was no 'British view' about international affairs, in the sense of a united outlook. What some historians do is to think that the 'British view' is expressed by members of the Foreign Office, just as they imagine they have studied 'British Foreign Policy' by reading the rot that Foreign Office officials turned out. Most of the time, this bears no relation to anything. Sometimes it bears a relation to the narrow, self-centred views of a few diplomats who imagine they belong to the upper classes. The 'British view' can also be interpreted as meaning the view of the British Cabinet, or of its leading members. In one sense, the 'British view' is in the last resort the view taken by the Prime Minister, because he or she is in a better position than anyone else to operate it – or thinks he/she is.

But the 'British view' has a new aspect nowadays. Until recently, our sources of information have been predominantly from the Foreign Office and – to a lesser extent – records of other civilian government departments. But now we have the records of the Chiefs of Staff Committee, and there emerges a British view which rests on current military opinion – something again quite different from the other kinds of British view. Opinions are sometimes deliberately formulated by the Chiefs of Staff in order to influence the Prime Minister, and do not necessarily represent their pure views. The real Chiefs of Staff opinions

40

are sometimes concealed from the Prime Minister and the Cabinet, because the effect of such opinions would be regrettable from the point of view of the Chiefs of Staff. Opinions, for example, are mostly expressed with extreme emphasis, in order to get larger army, navy or air estimates. The main concern of any Chief of Staff is that more money should be spent on whatever service he is running, and preferably less money on another service. Nevertheless, there is such a thing as a Chiefs of Staff point of view.

There is another kind of British view: the opinions expressed in the newspapers. Different newspapers, of course, have contradictory views, but there is one useful piece of advice which should be given to anyone who is thinking of studying public opinion: that at no time are the newspapers reliable reflections of public opinion. The students of views expressed in newspapers should ask themselves certain questions. Do newspapers try to influence public opinion; or do they try to express public opinion; or does the editor worry mainly about filling up the columns next morning? I have had long experience with newspapermen, and every editor I have known was not interested in policy, was not interested in war and peace, but was dominated by the fact that before seven o'clock at night, his front page had got to be set up. What goes into that front page depends on what news has come in. And, finally, there is yet another possible meaning of 'British view'. It may mean, in a vague, impressionistic way, the sort of outlook which ordinary people had at the time.

Whichever of these various things we consider to be the British view, there are certain general observations which may be made. August 1939 was a comparatively relaxed period. By contrast, the previous year's affairs – certainly September 1938, and perhaps the whole period from the May crisis onwards – were marked by apprehension in all the various circles discussed: apprehension by the diplomats, the Ministers, the Chiefs of Staff, the newspapers, and by ordinary people. The symbolic episode of early September 1938 – preceding by just a month the expected outbreak of war – was the digging of trenches in Hyde Park. How they would have worked as air raid shelters, I don't know. Perhaps it was intended that Hyde Park should be defended from the German invader. Yet trenches in Hyde Park – or postal delivery of gas masks – such things were the symbols of the apprehension of 1938.

August 1939 was quite different. People went on holiday in a perfectly normal way. They didn't worry that maybe something was going to happen. They had lived in a state of crisis for practically the whole of the preceding twelve months, and therefore much of the tension had evaporated. If you live in a crisis long enough, of course you get used to it, and it isn't a crisis any more. Even the earlier tension in 1939, which accompanied the guarantee to Poland, had nothing like the same effect as the tension of 1938. It was seen as a political event, and the outlook of people to such events had changed fundamentally in the period since the Czech crisis and Munich.

In 1938 there was deep apprehension of war. I addressed quite a number of meetings in the week or two before the Munich conference and they were the hardest meetings I ever addressed. I was always greeted by the argument: 'What you say means war and we don't want it'. Yet at the same time there was a profound feeling that the cause of Czechoslovakia was a just cause. All my friends and colleagues believed passionately that Czechoslovakia was a democratic state, the only one left in central Europe – and that it was the duty of the rest of the powers to save Czechoslovakia. I was in the embarrassing situation of knowing a great deal more than most of them about Czech policy, and particularly of appreciating that Czechoslovakia presented one of the outstanding examples of a nationality incorporated in a state against its will. I recognised that there were three million Germans wanting to leave Czechoslovakia; so my argument was always purely practical. It was desirable that we should defeat Hitler – even if this meant compelling three million Germans to stay in Czechoslovakia, and shooting any who tried to get away. This was correct; but it was not necessarily moral.

In March 1939, with the British guarantee to Poland, there was apparently a decisive stand, by contrast with what had happened for most of the previous year. Before the crisis of September 1938, the British Government had refused to involve itself, or pledge itself to involvement, in European affairs, beyond its strictly defensive alliance with France. The British guarantee to Poland involved repudiation of the idea of keeping out of Europe, and also an implied repudiation of the widely held idea that some of Poland's possessions were unjustified. Whereas people would have hesitated and found it difficult to decide what was the correct line to take over Czechoslovakia in a moral sense, nearly all British people would have said that the establishment of Danzig – a city inhabited almost entirely by Germans – as a Free City was wrong, and that the Corridor was also unjust to Germany. More than this, they did not feel that Poland represented the sort of democratic community which Czechoslovakia, allegedly, had done. Thus the Polish issue was not one which commanded the same sort of moral support as the issue of Czechoslovakia had done. British people, I think, accepted the guarantee to Poland as something that the Government had thought necessary. It had come just after the German occupation of Prague, and it was very desirable, in British eyes, to give some sort of response to indicate that British feelings were not altogether dead. Hitler had cheated over the occupation of western Czechoslovakia and an answer was required. The appropriate answer happened to be the guarantee to Poland; but what the British people welcomed was the answer and not the guarantee.

When there was no immediate German move against Poland, then it seemed that the guarantee had done its work. That, at least, was the view of ordinary people. To the Chiefs of Staff, the situation was different. They recognised that the guarantee was in existence; but as they were totally unable to fulfil that guarantee, they did not consider it as a factor in British strategy. The British, on the outbreak of war, would doubtless give Poland their blessing and perhaps they would even make some gesture in the West; but nobody ever contemplated fulfilling that guarantee except purely in terms of gesture.

The whole matter of the guarantee faded during the summer of 1939, because from the time it was issued down to August there was no immediate apprehension of a German attack. There was talk of German advances in armaments, but there was no striking mobilisation, as there had been against the Czechs. The Poles, on their side, remained arrogantly confident, refusing to make any concession to their allies or guarantors. Later, when Poland had been overrun, she became something of a moral cause – though always a contested one; but Poland had little of this moral weight in the summer of 1939. Thus, despite the outcry over the German occupation of Prague, and the transformation of western Czechoslovakia into a German protectorate, there were few alarms thereafter. In fact, there were no anxieties until the beginning of August.

It is true that there was talk that the Germans would do

something later. It had almost become a rule that in autumn, Germany would commit some act of aggression — just as there used to be a rule before 1914 which said, 'When the snow melts on the Balkan mountains, there will be war'. In much the same way there was gradually growing up a rule which said that around September each year, Hitler — as it were — emerges from his summer sleep and becomes troublesome. Maybe, when we all enjoyed the summer of 1939, it was because we all half-knew that something would happen after that.

Following on the guarantee to Poland, there was a demand from various sources for an alliance with Russia. Some of that demand came from a practical consideration, endorsed by the Chiefs of Staff: that the only way to aid Poland was by such an alliance, because there was no other route of access to Poland. As realistically minded people, the Chiefs of Staff saw that only Russia could provide an adequate fighting force to turn the scale on the eastern front.

With some people there was a moral or idealistic side to this desire for an alliance with Russia. In the early 1930s Russia had represented utopia, or something like it, for many people on the left. There had followed an increasing estrangement, beginning in 1936 or perhaps earlier, because of the purge trials and then the mass murders of the Stalinist regime. By 1939, Soviet Russia had lost most of the moral appeal it had once had for people on the left or even in the liberal centre. Yet if Russia could be brought back — as it were — into respectability, then she could become an ally and take on the main burden of the war against Germany, through giving aid to Poland.

It is quite true that this was an impossible proposition. Perhaps the Russians were unwilling; but the decisive factor, in August 1939, was that the Poles were more than unwilling — they were utterly determined not to accept Soviet aid on any conditions whatsoever. This fact — insofar as it was known — led to what one might call a slump in the Polish moral stock (which had never been very high) and to a corresponding rise in the Soviet stock. However, there was a much more practical consideration. Although the apprehensions which existed in March 1939 were less than those which had existed in 1938, they were reduced further by the prospect — held out all through the negotiations of the early summer of 1939 — that an alliance would be achieved with Soviet Russia. I can remember at that time living in lodgings in Oxford with an elderly lady of slightly aristocratic background – certainly of impeccably Conservative views. I can remember her opening her *Daily Mail*, and then singing along the passage, 'We've got an alliance with Russia, we've got an alliance with Russia!' Russia suddenly became, no longer a Red country, but a powerful name which would do all the fighting for us. The lack of anxiety of ordinary people in the summer of 1939 sprang partly from the delusion that a Soviet alliance would be achieved, and that it would be massively effective. Hence the feeling of re-laxation was very great.

For all these reasons, there was in 1939 none of the extreme pressure on the Government which there had been in 1938. Maybe that pressure had come from a minority, but it was still pressure, and it derived from the feeling that something must be done for the Czechs. That pressure had strongly harassed the Prime Minister, because he thought it was a mistake. It had been strongly voiced by at any rate a minority in the Cabinet, and it had provided the cause of a rift which cut right across parties, and indeed right into private life. There was no such conflict in 1939. The guarantee had been given to Poland and there was no point in debating whether it should have been given or not. Poland was not a popular cause in the sense that Czechoslovakia had been. Speaking from memory, I don't think there was a single march down Whitehall between March and September 1939 in which people carried banners saying 'Stand by Poland'. At the last minute, that cry was raised in the House of Commons – but that was something quite different. It was not a symbol of popular pressure. Indeed, there weren't many popular pressures at all in the summer of 1939: it was a very agreeable, relaxed time; and not least for the British Government, now that the decision to give the guarantee to Poland had been taken.

Some 'experts' – I use that laughable term to describe some members of the Foreign Office – some 'experts' insisted that Hitler was insatiable, that he was preparing a new war for the autumn and that the lull was very dangerous. A good deal of material to that effect was fed into the British Foreign Office by Germans who opposed Hitler's policies. By 'opponents' of Hitler's policies I do not mean the real opposition (if it ever existed) but German Generals and administrators who feared that in a great war the Germans would be defeated. There is a very good case in point on this – and a terrible warning it is, too, to scholars. On 23 May, in a document which was first submitted at Nuremberg and which later appeared in the *Documents on German Foreign Policy*, it was stated that Hitler held a conference in Berlin, at which he said: 'War is certain; my will is implacable. It will be ruthless, and it will be a war not confined to Poland but it will include the Western Powers, and will lead to decisive victory or decisive defeat.' This document almost immediately reached the British Foreign Office and was then quoted by Vansittart. It was only quite recently that some enquiring scholar looked at the list of names of those said to be attending the conference, and checked up where they were. Out of the nine people said to be present, eight were not present. This could be checked from German newspapers: they were at other meetings, right across Germany. The document was a pure fabrication, but I was taken in by it, and quoted it in a book of mine until the book reached its seventh edition, when I had to put in a footnote saying 'All this is wrong'.

Except for this spurious record, a firm decision for war by Hitler cannot be documented until 23 August, when there were other reasons why he should have made that decision. But with the British Foreign Office this kind of document, and other information even less reliable on its face, was very effective. There was a constant stream of secret warnings from people like Weizsäcker, the German Under-Secretary of State, who didn't like Hitler's line. Quite apart from these warnings, of course, the leaders of British policy formation, particularly Chamberlain and Halifax, appreciated that the situation was very unstable. They took, or believed they had taken, some precautions. Rearmament was increased, or rather the plans for future rearmament were increased. British armaments in September 1939 were not markedly greater than they had been at the beginning of the year; but on the other hand factories were being prepared and the production of greater weapons was being organised – so much so, indeed, that by 1940 the RAF was able to win the Battle of Britain, largely with new aircraft.

At the same time, Chamberlain refused to believe that war was inevitable. The problem was to strike a balance between too much threatening of Hitler and too much conciliation. This was very awkward, for concession of Hitler's claims to Poland, as to Czechoslovakia, could be defended not only from a practical point of view, but also from a moral point of view. Many British people, including the Foreign Office and the leading Ministers, recognised that Hitler's current aims, so far as he had them, coincided exactly with what the British thought was right. It was not until practically the end of August 1939 that Hitler laid down in specific terms what he was demanding from Poland. As you may remember, Hitler never negotiated directly with Poland from the middle of March 1939 until the day before the outbreak of war; and in this sense his claims were never documented. But on 29 August – when he put them down – he said that what he desired from Poland was the incorporation of Danzig into Germany and a plebiscite in the Polish Corridor. One of the British diplomats at the Foreign Office minuted, 'but this we have already endorsed'. Unfortunately, the Poles had not endorsed it. This was to create great difficulties at the last moment.

However, there is a great deal more to it than that. British foreign policy had followed two conflicting lines right from the time that Hitler came to power. One was the line of resistance: to advocate some sort of alliance and external co-operation to block Hitler. The increase in armaments, though it moved very slowly until 1936, corresponded with the line of resistance. The other line was that of conciliation, based on the view (quite wrong in my opinion) that all the evil qualities of Nazism sprang from the harsh economic conditions in which Germany was living, and that once the Germans became prosperous they would forget all that rot which Hitler had been talking to them. On this view, a stable, prosperous Germany in the heart of Europe was essential for the prosperity of Europe as a whole.

There was another consideration. The last thing that the rulers of Britain wanted was to be in association with Soviet Russia. If only Hitler would become more normal, more moderate, more co-operative, then he would be welcome as an ally and become chief guardian of what was called 'European civilisation' against Soviet barbarism. Fear of Russia was a very strong theme in British policy, particularly in the Conservative Party, though not there alone. Indeed, when you get to the actual records of the war, you will find that the leading Labour Ministers – Attlee, and to a lesser extent, Bevin – were far more anti-Soviet than ever Churchill was.

Thus there were considerable arguments for conciliating Germany. Right up to the day of the occupation of Prague, the Board of Trade was much more active in this than the Foreign Office, who didn't like conciliation and appeasement. The Board of Trade, by contrast, was preparing detailed methods of co-operation with Germany, particularly in the Balkans but also on a wider scale. This was the first time that the Common Market raised its deleterious head. These negotiations were resumed in the early summer of 1939. Wohltat, who was Göring's economic operator, came to England where he and Sir Horace Wilson discussed matters in detail. Wohltat worked closely with Göring, and Göring was always a man against war. Right up to the last minute, he hoped to gain what he wanted without war. What happened to those negotiations in the last days of peace is a very obscure subject; but it seems fairly clear that they got to the point of formulating a precise deal in the latter days of July 1939. Hudson, a Minister at the Board of Trade, proposed a thousand million pound loan to Germany, in order to enable her to stabilise her civilian as well as her military industry. There is a very curious thing about this, for the story was leaked by Hudson himself. Now, did he leak it because he was so proud of what he had done? Did he leak it because he was an imbecile and did not appreciate its significance? Or did he leak it – as the few people who are favourable to Hudson have sometimes suggested – because he wanted to wreck it? For certainly it was representative of one aspect of British policy: the hope that current tension could be overcome.

There are other factors to consider. Some members of the British Government, including the Prime Minister, attached much more importance to the affairs of the Far East than they did to those of Europe. After all, Europe is composed of faraway countries of which we know nothing, whereas the Far East is an adjunct of the British Empire, or was in those days. The Far East had been the main practical anxiety of the British ever since the Manchurian crisis of 1931. Sometimes the Ministers hoped to get back on better terms with Japan. Sometimes they were restrained from this by pressure from America. By 1938, the British had other considerations which made them extremely anxious to avoid war in Europe, and particularly a war in the Mediterranean: they wanted to send what was called the Main Fleet to Singapore. Essential to the British concern for the Far East was the need to co-operate with the United States. The difficulty about this was that the basis of Anglo-American co-operation – in the Far East as elsewhere – was that the British should take action and the American Government would applaud. That is what

President Roosevelt said himself. 'Yes,' he said, 'I entirely approve your policy. I hope you go further, you've greatly enhanced our admiration for British policy.'

That is what the Americans offered. There was, all along, the belief that if only the British would do enough, then the Americans would do a bit more than approve. They might even send their fleet to the Far East – even though they would not use it when it got there. Furthermore, the pound, though stronger than it had been in 1931, was very much dependent on the American dollar and therefore American lack of disapproval was quite enough from certain points of view. Yet the British Government were in this awkward position, that both Roosevelt and the Dominion Premiers said, in effect, 'If we are to support you, then you must show, by greater resolution and action, that you are worth supporting'. Then, when the British did something to show that they were worth supporting, the Americans and the Dominions said, 'The fact that you have taken this action without our support means that you don't need it'. This was an attitude which the Dominions continued until 3 September 1939 (although they later relinquished it) and which America continued until Pearl Harbor, or at any rate until the summer of 1941.

Just as America put pressure on Britain without meaning to support her, so the British put pressure on France. France, the British decided, should take a more resolute line, and should indicate that this time there would be war if Germany went further. Of course it was possible to remind the French that, whereas the British had given a guarantee of a limited kind to Poland, Poland was France's ally and France would lose all prestige if she did not go to the assistance of her ally. Whether the French really cared about this very much any longer is difficult to say. Certainly I think both Gamelin, the French Commander-in-Chief, and Bonnet, the Foreign Minister, were extremely anxious to jettison their Polish ally at the first opportunity. In fact, they could not think of any other course to pursue. There was also the prospect, which had leaked out in the press, of economic co-operation with Germany.

The other theme, which was also pursued in public, was negotiations for an alliance with Russia. There were many factors which produced these negotiations. There is much to be said for the view that when the Russians started them they really believed that something would be achieved thereby. The French were extremely anxious for a real alliance with Russia, resurrecting the Franco-Russian alliance which had been made in 1894, and which had done something to take the German pressure off France.

British public opinion, no doubt, wanted an alliance without thinking of the problems involved. For the Government, it was much more difficult. Some members, including the Prime Minister, were most dubious about the desirability of an alliance. Some, like Halifax, were anxious to give the impression that they were negotiating for an alliance, and had not made up their minds whether it was meant seriously or not. The negotiations in fact ran on for several months. For the outside world, and even for the Germans, those negotiations represented a sufficiently genuine possibility to create apprehension in Hitler's mind. Gradually the notion was formulated, as a key to British policy, that the essential thing was to keep those negotiations going. As long as they went on, Hitler could not be sure that they would fail. Unless he was sure that they would fail, he would probably not plunge into war, but would find less dangerous ways of achieving his ambitions. As the British, on their side, were anxious to sell out Poland, these ways could probably be arranged. No deal, but no break! As the detailed diplomatic negotiations went on without either, they became increasingly unconvincing, with the Russians saying that something practical should be done. It was a brilliant stroke by the British, therefore, to decide that a military delegation should be sent out. While it was on its way there, on a slow boat, the negotiations still existed. Once it got there, you could settle down to equally prolonged negotiations – discussing in general terms military plans and so on.

So the delegations, British and French, went in. The British played things very well indeed. The first day of the negotiations with the Russians was interrupted by a question from Voroshilov: 'Where are your credentials?' The French had brought their credentials with them. But the British General had to say, 'I'm frightfully sorry, I think I left them in the club'. Two days were spent in wiring London, saying, 'Please send us credentials'. Where they were to be delivered is obscure. However that may be, the negotiations proved to be the dynamite which exploded the Second World War. On the third day, when the Russians enquired what was involved and realised that they were not going to be allowed to take part in a great war – that they were not going to have freedom to go against Germany in the way which they thought appropriate – the negotiations broke down.

Hitler again seized his opportunity. That all sprang from one single thing: now that negotiations had broken down, the entire concept of an alliance between the Western powers and Russia disappeared with them. From this collapse came the Russo-German Non-Aggression Pact of 23 August 1939.

At the time, there was a great outcry about the Nazi–Soviet pact. That pact did two things from the Russian point of view. It gave a guarantee of neutrality which was exactly what the British had been insisting on all along: that Russia should remain neutral, unless Poland asked her to join in – which the Poles had made clear they would not do. Thus Russia promised to the Germans the neutrality which the British wanted. The second thing that the pact provided was that, if Poland collapsed, those territories then under Poland which had a mixed population consisting partly of Poles, but also partly of Ukrainians and Byelorussians, would be 'liberated' and put under Russia. It is difficult to see what else the Russians could have done, unless they just sat back and hoped that nothing would happen.

At any rate, the pact completely transformed the political atmosphere in England. The mainstay, the great hope, of British policy had been that the negotiations with Russia could be prolonged. This was suddenly removed and the immediate reaction – impulsive and yet perfectly comprehensible – was to emphasise for the first time what the guarantee to Poland really amounted to: that is, to regard the Polish claims to the Corridor and to rights over Danzig as valid, and to declare an intention to go to war if necessary on the side of Poland. When the Anglo-Polish alliance was formally concluded on 25 August, it contained a clause which the British had hitherto rejected: that any German action over Danzig (which was not, after all, Polish territory) would be regarded as German aggression against Poland, and would set in motion the British obligation to go to war under that treaty. In this way, in resentment against what the Russians had done, the British abandoned all their reservations and were rushed over to the Polish side. It was only from this moment that Poland became something of an inspiration; the martyr which Czechoslovakia had been in the previous year.

Whatever could have been said about the situation in the past – that Britain should or should not have supported some small country or other – the sudden danger to Poland did bring out a clearer moral issue, for a definite promise had been given. Though it is rash to talk of 'public opinion' as a defined thing, it is very tempting to say that from 25 August 'public opinion' – meaning the opinion of Members of Parliament and in a wider sense the opinion of the general public – accepted the view that this promise must be honoured. Not that the general public was bubbling over with enthusiasm for Poland, or knew anything about her; but in a grumpy way they would say, 'Well, we have given our word, we must stick to it'. No promise had been made to Czechoslovakia before the crisis of September 1938; but a promise had been made to Poland and this proved a very powerful factor. For the Government it was, of course, an embarrassment. The moment that the promise had been given to Poland, the British Government set out, not to tear it up, but at any rate to withdraw from it and get back to a state of negotiations. From 25 August onwards, there was a series of visits by Dahlerus, a Swedish businessman who was an agent of Göring and acted as an intermediary to make a peaceful settlement possible.

The debate, unofficial as it was, between the British and German Governments (with Hitler himself directing affairs from a distance), was really centred on a quite simple point. The Poles had refused to negotiate with the Germans. They said there was nothing to negotiate about. All they wanted was to keep their national territory, which included the Corridor, and to keep their rights over Danzig, so there wasn't anything to discuss. The British Government held out an offer that they would induce the Poles to negotiate, if the German claims were moderate. Hitler replied, more than once, that his only claims were for Danzig and the Corridor but, as head of a Great Power he was not going to humiliate himself and put forward these claims as humble requests in order to please the Poles. If the Poles would send a delegation to Berlin in order to hear his demands, they would receive them. The Poles replied, 'If Hitler first of all drops his demands, we will send a delegation to Berlin'. This was the situation which the British tried to break down towards the end of August, when negotiations finally collapsed.

There was, until the end, an equivocation, a double line of

policy: one accepting war, the other seeking to maintain peace. I pass no judgement between them; but the policy of conciliation contributed to war in this way. When the British had pressed so strongly that they were not opposed to righteous German claims, it was only natural that Hitler on his side should assume that the British would not back Poland in a war which broke out over Danzig and the Corridor. On 25 August he first announced his intention of going to war, or rather issued his orders for war that day. He backed down when the Anglo-Polish alliance was announced, and then renewed his decision to go to war when the British emissaries were knocking at the door, offering him British support to get Polish agreement. With the German invasion on 1 September, the Poles at once asked for implementation of the guarantee.

# 4 The French View

**Douglas Johnson**

Professor Donald Watt has observed that the British 'growth industry' in discussing events of 1939 has not been paralleled by a similar development in France. There appear to be three reasons for this.

The first reason is rather technical. French official policy towards archives has been very restrictive; and furthermore some of the most important records probably no longer exist. In Winston Churchill's history of the Second World War,[1] he describes his last visit to the Quai d'Orsay in 1940, when he learnt of the gloomy situation on the war front. Churchill looked out of the window on a very beautiful summer day and saw gentlemen in neat suits, who had just removed their jackets. These men were busily engaged in burning the archives in preparation for the oncoming German invasion. Professor Renouvin, the French expert who has done much to push forward the study of his country's diplomacy during this period, describes another incident during this destruction process. He also went to the Quai d'Orsay and saw volumes being hurriedly burned. One fell at his feet: the file of correspondence between Paris and Berlin in 1928. The contents of that volume, so it happens, were not lost irretrievably, for a copy of the same material was found in Berlin at the end of the war and was seized by the British. Thereafter it was edited – probably by Professor Watt or one of his colleagues – and subsequently published.[2] Quite a lot of the Quai d'Orsay documents were duplicated in the archives of various French embassies abroad and many of these have since been published; but others have been lost irretrievably.

The second reason for the dearth of French historiography about 1939 is perhaps more interesting. For Frenchmen, 1939 is not the date which requires investigation. The date which matters to them is 1940. That was the year of the defeat, the armistice

54

and the occupation; and in that year emerge several new phenomena in French politics. In 1940 was established the Vichy state, *l'Etat Français*: that interruption in a succession of republics. 1940 saw the beginning of the resistance movement: a completely new kind of movement in French history, closely associated with General de Gaulle. Thus it is 1940 rather than 1939 which has been the great focus of French re-examination.

The third reason is perhaps more significant than either of the other two. To some people who have sought to view 1939 from the French angle, it has appeared that France did not have the initiative; that French diplomacy of the period was of secondary importance, because France was the prisoner of external events. Political geography prescribed that there was only one possible enemy for France and that was Germany. Economic geography precluded France from taking the lead in dealing with Germany, for France was not a heavily industrialised state. Demography led to the same conclusion, for France was underpopulated. The psychology of the French people was dominated by recollections of what had happened between 1914 and 1918, which powerfully underlined the fact that France was in desperate need of allies. After all, in the earlier war it only proved possible to defeat Germany because France had at some time or other possessed the three most powerful allies in the world: the United Kingdom, Russia and the United States of America. Even with these great allies, victory had only been achieved at the cost of four years of occupation in ten departments of northern France, of enormous devastation and a terrible loss of life.

In some important respects, France's situation was worse than it had been in 1914, and her bargaining position in relation to potential allies was weaker. In 1914, France had had considerable strength as a capitalist power which was able to lend money to other countries, and thereby sometimes to exert considerable influence over their policies. The Franco-Russian alliance, which had been so important in 1914, was founded upon French loans to Russia. No corresponding possibilities were open to France in 1938 and 1939 in relation to Soviet Russia. After Munich, the one reliable continental ally of France – Czechoslovakia – had been abandoned. The Stresa Front, and other attempts to make Italy an ally, had failed. The French were disposed to view other actual or potential links with foreign powers with considerable scepticism. They had never had much faith in the League of Nations. In spite of Aristide Briand, they had little confidence in the Locarno agreement. They knew that there could be no complete alliance with the United Kingdom. In the 1920s and early 1930s, it had been possible for French statesmen like Poincaré or Briand or Barthou to hold the initiative in world affairs; but by the late 1930s that initiative had been lost. France could only follow Britain; and therefore French diplomacy in this period is not a subject of very great interest to most present-day French historians.

That is the common view; but I think that it is now being revised. Robert J. Young, a student of Donald Watt, has made some contributions to this revision in a recent book[3] – even though he did not have access to the French archives. A further book has now appeared, written by Professor Duroselle, who did have this access; a book entitled *La Décadence*,[4] which covers the period of French diplomacy from 1932 to 1939. Two major French statesmen of the period have necessarily been the subjects of considerable rethinking by such writers – just as there has been much rethinking in this country about Neville Chamberlain. The first of the French statesmen is Edouard Daladier, who not only was Prime Minister in 1939, but who also occupied a particularly dominant political position. Daladier had been Minister of Defence since 1936, and therefore he had been closely connected with the problem of French security for an unusually long period for a politician in his country. It is customary to see him as a man who was apparently strong and obstinate yet was in reality weak. All sorts of witticisms have been passed about the real nature of the 'Bull of Vaucluse', as he was called. The horns of the bull, it was said, were in reality the horns of a snail; behind the aggressive exterior was a very weak politician. I think that now we see him as a man who was very well respected and much admired; an accomplished and able politician, who was wielding enormous power within the framework of French government. It was difficult for Frenchmen to imagine anybody replacing Daladier; and that was a very important political fact at the time. Undoubtedly he had both resolution and prudence. He was a man of great introspection; a man who thought and meditated a great deal.

The other French politician of the time who has now come in for considerable re-examination is Daladier's Foreign Minister, Georges Bonnet, who, like his chief, was a member of the Radical

Party. Bonnet was undoubtedly a very able man. He had been a soldier, a civil servant, he had served in various Ministries, and had been Ambassador to the United States. Perhaps it is important to bear in mind the nature of the Radical Party for our assessment of both Daladier and Bonnet. That party combined different threads: the Radicals believed in the State; yet, at the same time, they believed in the small man – the individual, who had a right to independence. Therefore there is a certain fluidity in the position of the Radical Party and, indeed, in any Radical politician. It is true that Bonnet was a manipulator, very keen to retain power. His wife was also very keen on this power, and became known as 'Soutien-Georges' because of the determination with which she supported her husband. Unlike Chamberlain, Bonnet survived the war and spent a long time thereafter defending his actions of the 1930s.

The sort of dilemma which France faced during the period just before the War was epitomised in her experiences in 1938, the year of the Munich agreement. The French had two very different objectives. First, they wanted to support their ally, Czechoslovakia; but, second, they wanted to strengthen their British alliance. The only way in which they could increase Britain's commitment to France was by decreasing their own commitment to Czechoslovakia. France faced other difficulties of an internal character. Within the Government there was a group, headed by the Minister of Finance, Paul Reynaud, which was prepared to support France going to war. Then there was Georges Bonnet, who was opposed to having any war at all – and between them stood Daladier. He sought to keep his Government together, as any Prime Minister must do; but he also had his own distinctive attitude to the danger of war. He believed that France must accept the challenge of war if it was forced upon her by Germany; but he also believed that there should not be a war if it was a matter of French choice.

Military considerations also played their part in France's dilemma. The French Generals were in favour of a war in which Germany would have to fight on two fronts – one of those fronts against the Czech army – but they were opposed to a major confrontation on the French frontier. A further military consideration also operated. It was recognised that air power was very important and that hostile air power could destroy the nation; but the French air force was weak. Nor could one exclude politics from the calculations. There was a widespread belief that if there were a European war, this would lead to an increase in the power of Communism. It is important in this connection to remember that the French Parliament of 1939, upon which the current Government depended, was the same Parliament which had been elected in 1936, and had for a time sustained in office the Popular Front. During the lifetime of that current Parliament, there had been, from 1936 to 1938, the greatest wave of strikes that France had ever known. Many people in that period believed that France was in imminent danger of a Communist revolution: a danger which would be increased further by war.

Such was the background; but in 1939 a number of changes had begun. As Donald Watt has mentioned, the idea began to be put about that Germany was contemplating a move against Great Britain, perhaps preceded by a move against Holland and Belgium, rather than a move against France. If that was the case, then France might well be able to stand by and allow that to happen. She could then do a deal with Hitler, or Mussolini, or both. It is difficult to distinguish between the the real elements advanced in support of this theory and the false elements. There is no doubt that real elements existed, but other elements were invented. Many of the military details originated in the *Deuxième Bureau*, and came from French Intelligence sources. This *Deuxième Bureau* was a sort of French 'dirty tricks' department which was trying to push the British Government to act in closer correspondence with French wishes and interests. British diplomats recognised this, but nevertheless felt that there was a basis of truth in the argument.

At the beginning of 1939, Britain moved into a dilemma which was not unlike the French dilemma of 1938. Just as Britain was France's most valuable ally, so was France Britain's most valuable ally. Britain was constrained to encourage the French – to assure them that the British were committed to the French, in order that France should not make a separate deal. While Britain was bound to keep France as her ally, she must also try to discourage the French from doing anything foolish. All this must be operated in relation to a French system which the British statesmen and diplomats never really understood; but insofar as they did understand it, they viewed it with the greatest of contempt. Their despatches, their private letters, all show this patronising attitude to French politicians – which must have been unbearable to the French, so far as they were aware of it.

The British furthermore appreciated that the French situation was not only complex, but also subject to the possibility of dramatic change in the near future: for another general election was due in France in 1940. What sort of Parliament, what sort of Government, would succeed the Parliament of 1936 and the Governments which it kept in office?

In the course of 1939, the French Government adopted three lines of approach to military and diplomatic questions. First, they began negotiations with Poland. The Polish Minister of War visited Paris in May and discussed matters with the French High Command, including General Gamelin, Chief of the National Defence Staff. Gamelin decided on a plan of action, should Poland be invaded by Germany. France would take immediate air action against the Germans; then, on the third day of the German invasion of Poland, the French army would commence limited military action against Germany. On the fifteenth day, the French army would engage the Germans with the greater part of its forces. Yet, in spite of this agreement, there was no real planning. The Polish General Staff did not tell the French what their war plans were and the French did not tell theirs to the Poles. After that meeting of May 1939 there was not further military consultation between the French and the Poles. When the Quai d'Orsay learned of those military discussions, they were indignant. They had always viewed with the greatest apprehension the whole idea of French intervention in the case of a German war against Poland. The French ambassador to Poland had deliberately played down any suggestion that he would discuss what the French might do should the Germans attack. Thereafter, the situation changed. General Gamelin wrote to his Polish counsellor to say that the military agreement depended upon a general political agreement between France and Poland. That general agreement never took place; but private, secret negotiations were started between Bonnet and the Polish ambassador in Warsaw; negotiations of which the French ambassador in Warsaw knew nothing.

The second line of approach which the French Government adopted in 1939 was to look closely at the Rome–Berlin Axis. Manifestly, Italy was the weaker partner; therefore, in event of war, the French and British should concentrate their efforts on attacking Italy. The French had many ideas as to what should happen in the Mediterranean. In August a meeting took place between the French navy chief, Admiral Darlan, and the British representative, Sir Dudley Pound, at Portsmouth, and these ideas were discussed. The British were much taken aback to learn that the French proposed action against Spain, and even for moving into Greece. This scheme is to be explained not only by the logic of the situation, but also by the fact that the French wanted the war to be fought in the Mediterranean or elsewhere – not, as in 1914, on French soil.

The third element which entered French calculations was the view that any war would be a very long one. This was to the advantage of Britain and France, who would become relatively stronger by comparison with their adversaries as the conflict proceeded.

It is not necessary to stress the evident fact that all those themes of French policy failed. In the first place Poland was rapidly overcome and divided between Germany and Soviet Russia. In the second place, there was no question of concentrating the war effort against Italy, because Italy chose to be non-belligerent. In the third place – so far as France was concerned – the war was not a long one, but moved rapidly to an end in May and June 1940.

The whole of French diplomatic thinking really collapsed in ruins with the signature of the German–Soviet pact on 23 August 1939. Thereafter, French diplomacy became extraordinarily inactive, in sharp contrast with the diplomacy of the British or the Poles. Many Frenchmen at first did not think that the German–Soviet pact represented a definitive change in Soviet policy. The French military attaché in Moscow declared that it was a temporary move on the part of the Soviets, a *pis aller*. There is evidence that many important French politicians took the same view. At the same time, Bonnet expressed the opinion that it was by no means certain that there would be British support for Poland, should the Germans invade. Both the judgement about Russia and the judgement about Britain disposed the French to inaction, because they were by no means sure that the crisis was coming. Meanwhile, a very important group of French people – the French appeasers, if one wishes so to call them – became extremely active in suggesting that there was no reason why France should find herself at war as a result of the likely international events. On 25 August, Hitler aimed his diplomatic weapon at this group, by explaining that the Germans had no ideas of aggression against France, and had given up the idea that they ever wished to occupy Alsace and Lorraine in the future. At this time Daladier made an appeal for peace in a private letter to Hitler, to which he attached great importance. The French Government meanwhile devoted much attention to discussing whether the Germans were not, in fact, bluffing in their threat to bring about an invasion of Poland.

French diplomacy became extremely active again from 31 August onwards. A new idea was launched in a conversation between the Italian Foreign Minister, Count Ciano and the French ambassador, François-Poncet – a man whose reputation was very considerable. The Italian Government wished to organise a conference to discuss the future of Poland; in other words, to produce a repetition of Munich. A date – 5 September – was even mentioned. On learning about the conversation, the French Foreign Minister, Bonnet, moved into considerable activity in order to follow up the idea of a conference. The Prime Minister, Daladier, was at first opposed to this, but at times he hesitated, since he wished to keep his Government together.

At twenty past eight in the morning of 1 September, France learned officially that the Germans had invaded Poland; yet it was not until five o'clock in the afternoon of 3 September that the French declared war in support of Poland, which had been their ally since 1921. Furthermore, this French declaration of war took place six hours after the British declaration of war. Clearly there had been some attempt by French statesmen to delay things.

One reason for that delay was military, for General Gamelin required it. Yet it was Bonnet who used the Italian suggestion of a conference in order to avert any definite, irrevocable step towards war. The course of events during this short, but crucial, period may now be studied hour by hour and, indeed, telephone call by telephone call. It has been suggested by Professor Duroselle and others that here we see not only a different diplomatic appraisal, but a clash of mentality, a clash almost of social attitudes, between the British and French Governments. Some people in the British Conservative Party (and, indeed, some in the Labour and Liberal Parties) felt doubts about the wisdom of a guarantee to Poland; but once this guarantee had been given, they thought it should be sustained. In France, however – and particularly in the Radical Party – the very different tradition of French diplomacy is demonstrated. One never gave up; it was necessary to look at every treaty not as an overwhelming moral obligation, but as something which required to be studied, something which had to be negotiated. It was always said that a treaty was only valuable in accordance with the value of its escape clauses.

Following such precepts, Bonnet began to engage in a series of manoeuvres. He acted as if he had been given a *carte blanche* by the French Government – which was not the case. He ignored the British attitude and he ignored the fact of the invasion of Poland. He did not always keep the Prime Minister informed of his actions. A great many events now began to occur in different places. The Italian ambassador made contact with a relative who was a French nobleman. The prominent French politician, Pierre Laval, made contact with the Italian consul in Lyon. The Italian Government gave encouragement to such approaches. Count Ciano gave orders that the Italian newspapers should not attack France or the French people. French public opinion was grasping at the idea that there was a possibility that war might be avoided. Within the French Cabinet, the hard-liners tended to be isolated. Paul Reynaud, for example, was not leader of an important political group. Within the French Socialist Party, even, there were many people to be found who favoured an agreement. The Socialists in particular were acutely conscious of the dangers of Communism. On 2 September, when the French Chamber of Deputies met, General Gamelin asked for forty-eight hours' delay. Bonnet believed that if he could get that forty-eight hours' delay, he could get a conference and find a way out. There is evidence to show that he did not believe that Polish resistance would last for long, and in that sense he thought he was negotiating from a good position.

Meanwhile, other pressures were being exerted on the French Government from London. It was not true, as many people thought at the time, that Neville Chamberlain was trying to get out of his obligations. What Chamberlain was trying to do – and this is the important point – was to ensure that the Franco-British alliance was maintained, and that Britain did not find herself going to war in support of Poland without France at her side: an event which Britain greatly feared. At the same time, however, Britain had not made any arrangements to transfer the RAF to France. As Gamelin put it, 'They want us to declare war today, but they are only going to send their planes tomorrow'. Looking at the matter from the angle of his own service, the French naval commander, Admiral Darlan, did not understand why this declaration of war must take place so soon. It was therefore in an atmosphere of multiple suspicions and recriminations that Bonnet was eventually forced to recognise that the Italian idea of conferences would not materialise, and that he was therefore compelled to accept a declaration of war.

Such was the unpromising start to the wartime alliance. The French 'peace party' was not destroyed by the declaration of war on the evening of 3 September 1939. The events which we have studied had their bearing on others which lay in the future: the reluctance of the British Government to commit all its air forces to France in the early summer of 1940; perhaps the decision of the British Government to evacuate from Dunkirk, and later to give precedence to British rather than French soldiers in that evacuation; and then the French capitulation in June 1940. There would be reverberations later still: notably, the anti-British sentiment evinced by General de Gaulle, even as he led his small movement of intransigents in London. All these events are to be explained – in part at least – by the nature of the diplomatic events which took place in France in September 1939 and the preceding months.

## NOTES AND REFERENCES

1. Winston S. Churchill, *The Second World War*, (London, 1948, *et seq.*) vol. II p. 42.
2. *Akten zur Deutschen Auswärtigen Politik 1918–1945*, Serie B, 1925–33, vols VIII, IX, X (Göttingen, 1976).
3. Robert J. Young, *In Command of France: French Foreign Policy and Military Planning 1933–1940* (Cambridge, Mass. and London, 1978).
4. J.-B. Duroselle, *La Décadence, 1932–1939* (Paris, 1979).

# 5 The Polish View

**Józef Garliński**

Poles are more conscious of their country's history than many
people in the world. Unless we appreciate something of Poland's
more distant past, it is difficult or impossible to understand why
the Poles of 1939 acted as they did, and took the decisions which
they did.

The history of Poland began in the tenth century. After establishing her position in Central Europe as a liberal and Catholic
state, Poland entered into a union with Lithuania. 'Lithuania'
meant something far greater than the present Soviet Republic of
the same name, for it included much of what we now call White
Russia and a large part of the Ukraine as well. This union
between Poland and Lithuania was at first personal, and
achieved by the choice of a Lithuanian prince as King of Poland
in the fourteenth century. Later on, in the fifteenth century,
political union followed. This period – the fifteenth, sixteenth
and seventeenth centuries – was a time of expansion for Poland in
the east, and it saw the creation of an empire which comprised
many nations, and covered an area of over a million square kilometres.

Unfortunately, the large increase in area did not go hand
in hand with social and political reforms. Poland failed to
modernise its outdated system. The passage of a new measure
through Parliament was subject to the *Liberum veto*, whereby
any member of the House could block action. After the Jagiel-
lonian dynasty died out in the sixteenth century, there was a free
election for every new king with a great deal of foreign influence.
At the end of the eighteenth century Poland lost her independence. She was divided between Russia, Prussia and Austria, and
for over a hundred years struggled to return to political freedom.
After uprisings and every form of resistance, the Poles finally
achieved what they wanted at the end of the First World War,

when quite exceptional circumstances arose: all three partitioning powers were defeated. The Austro-Hungarian Empire had
collapsed, so the Poles had no problems from that direction.
Poland won a separate war against revolutionary Russia in
1919–20, and achieved a peace settlement in 1921 which decided
the frontiers between the two countries – although, of course,
Soviet Communism continued to sow disorder within Poland.
From Germany, Poland regained a part of Pomerania, a part of
Silesia and areas surrounding Poznań: a state of affairs which
angered German 'revisionists', who took every opportunity to
complain that the Poles had taken German territories.

The various races living in Poland – as in most of eastern and
central Europe – are so profoundly mixed that it was impossible
to establish any boundaries which did not include large numbers
of non-Poles within the Polish state; and, conversely, to leave
large numbers of Poles outside Poland. The new country covered
only 388 thousand square kilometres, and in 1939 had about
thirty-five million inhabitants. About 30 per cent of these
belonged to various minorities – among them three million Jews,
over three million Ukrainians, about one million Byelorussians,
700 thousand Germans and some others.

Although Poland signed a peace treaty with Russia and also
an arbitration pact with Germany, she was under constant threat
from both east and west. Each year, with the growing strength of
German revisionism and the organisation of the new post-revolu-
tionary order in Russia, both threats increased. The situation
became particularly serious when Hitler came to power and
began to set aside the articles of the Treaty of Versailles. In 1934
Poland signed a pact of non-aggression with Germany, which was
supposed to last for ten years; but Hitler's 'revisionist' plans went
so far that the value of that pact became of very little significance.

The Poles, who had at last achieved their freedom after so
many years of subjection, were determined to defend it at any
price. In this respect, all Poles were united. The Government of
1930 was a semi-dictatorship and that Government was by no
means universally popular; but in their determination to fight in
defence of national independence there were no differences
between Poles. This was well illustrated at the moment of the
German attack on 1 September 1939 when, held back by the
Western powers, and for other reasons, Poland was only able to

carry out partial mobilisation. The troops marching to the front were besieged by young reservists who had not been called up, and who begged to be given arms and taken into the ranks. I was myself a witness of such scenes as a young reserve Second Lieutenant of Cavalry, and I felt happy to be in uniform.

The general course of international events in 1938–9 is familiar enough. In March 1938, Austria was forcibly incorporated in the Third Reich. In September of that year, the decision was taken to give the Sudetenland to Germany. In the following March, German divisions moved into the Czechoslovak capital. The structure of Europe established at Versailles had been gravely undermined. Hitler now directed his gaze at Poland, and the Western powers – Great Britain and France – were forced to take a more active part in events. On 31 March 1939, Prime Minister Chamberlain announced in the House of Commons that Britain would give a military guarantee to Poland. This was a reversal of British policy, because for twenty years British Governments had refused to accept responsibility for the stability of eastern Europe. Of course, this commitment limited British freedom of manoeuvre in relations with Soviet Russia; but her attitude towards Germany and towards Poland was important, so Britain and France approached the Soviet Government and started negotiations. The Soviet attitude was clear. Certainly Russia might be interested in giving assistance to Poland if the latter were attacked by Hitler; but the Poles must agree to accept Soviet troops on Polish soil. Nothing came of these negotiations. Meanwhile, Hitler asked Stalin to receive von Ribbentrop and – to the amazement of the world – on 23 August the Soviet–German Pact of Non-Aggression – the Ribbentrop-Molotov Pact – was signed. One of its secret clauses provided for a new partition of Poland. The Poles did not know of this clause at the time, but they knew that any Russo-German agreement presented a deadly threat to Poland.

In theory, there had originally been four options open to Poland:

1. To accept all Hitler's demands.
2. To allow the Red Army to move into Polish territory.
3. To ignore the German demands, but also to refuse the guarantee offered by Britain.
4. To accept the guarantee and fight the Germans in the event of attack.

Today we know that Poland chose the fourth option, and we know the course of events which followed. It is useful, however, to consider what each of these options entailed, to decide in the light of present knowledge whether Poland was wise or not.

Hitler's demands on Poland contained two basic conditions: the return to the Reich of Gdańsk (Danzig), which was at that time a free city with certain Polish rights, and rail and road connections with East Prussia across Polish Pomerania. In return, the Germans proposed to prolong the pact of non-aggression to twenty-five years and to guarantee the Polish frontiers.

The Polish Government rejected these demands, and the whole nation stood behind it; for the Poles, after long years of subjection, were most sensitive on the matter of their independence. They reacted emotionally and would not consider any reduction of their rights. The German demands were considered outrageous. Such was the reaction of ordinary Poles; but the Government had to consider the matter from every point of view, and to think of the consequences of such a refusal. Were they right in reasoning in the same way?

The answer must be affirmative. It was already obvious that Hitler was playing a game, and that acceptance of his conditions gave no security. Poles recalled in particular what had happened in the matter of the Sudetenland and Czechoslovakia. At the conference in Munich at the end of September 1938, the Prime Ministers of Britain and France met Hitler and Mussolini and agreed that the Sudetenland should be incorporated into Germany and that Czechoslovakia should be given a guarantee of her new frontiers. The resolutions of the conference were carried out, but the guarantee proved worthless. The Germans secretly urged Czechoslovakia's neighbours to demand disputed territories from her. The Hungarians did so, as also, unfortunately, did the Poles, and Slovakia became independent. On 15 March 1939, German tanks rolled into Prague, ending the existence of independent Czechoslovakia and making it very obvious to all how much value could be placed on Hitler's guarantees and promises. If the Poles had agreed to Gdańsk being incorporated in the Reich, and to Pomerania being crossed by German lines of communication, this would only have been the first step towards the destruction of Polish independence.

The second option was to accept the Soviet proposals, and allow the Red Army on to Polish soil. This could have happened as the result of negotiations carried on in Moscow by missions sent from London and Paris, and thus with agreement and en-couragement from the Western Allies. It was not out of the question that a Soviet–Western agreement could have led to the complete encirclement of Germany, and this could have compelled Hitler to reflect and revise his war plans. Yet later events proved that Hitler and Stalin saw things otherwise. It is useful nevertheless to consider the problem from the Polish point of view and try to answer the question: could the Poles have agreed to this?

Once again we must return to the past and recall that Russia was one of the countries which annexed part of Poland, through the policies of Catherine II and her successors. Indeed, the rule of Russia was the most oppressive of all the three partitioning powers, and so the struggle for freedom in those parts was fiercest. Two great uprisings took place there and were bloodily suppressed. Because of this memory and experience, the Polish Government in rejecting the Soviet proposals was again acting with full support of the whole nation. The later events of the war – the partitioning of Poland between Germany and Russia in the autumn of 1939, the annexation of eastern Poland, and the domination of the whole of Poland by Russia which has con-tinued down to the present – have all confirmed how right this attitude had been. The rapacity of Russia, whether controlled by Whites or Reds, has always been the same from the Polish point of view.

The third option apparently open to Poland was to reject the German demands, and at the same time to decline with thanks the proffered British guarantee. The Germans were bound to consider acceptance of such guarantees to be a provocative act: Poland lining up with Germany's enemies, as it were. Hitler confirmed this by breaking off the pact of non-aggression with Poland as soon as he heard that the British offer had been accepted. Yet does it seem now, on mature reflection, that refusal could have made any difference to Hitler's plans of conquest, and could have saved Poland from a German attack? The answer is an emphatic negative. Hitler had written in *Mein Kampf*:

> We terminate the endless German drive to the South and West of Europe and direct our gaze towards the lands in the East . . .
> If we talk about new soil and territory in Europe today, we can think primarily only of Russia and its vassal border states.

For many years, few people outside Germany took *Mein Kampf* seriously, for people did not believe that there could exist a politician who would reveal in advance his plans – and such plans in particular. But when later it appeared that Hitler was carrying out word for word his early proposals, then the view that no kind of appeasement would have stopped the German dictator proved to be correct. Yet even if people could somehow discount *Mein Kampf* as the vapourings of an immature politician, which would become modified by experience in office, there was still ample evidence from other sources to show that such words did indeed embody Hitler's current intentions. German preparations in the early part of 1939 showed clearly that Hitler meant to start a war any month. The argument that the attack might have been in the west and not in the east if Poland had been more docile and had avoided provoking the German dictator, finds no confirmation from observed facts. The Germans were looking for *Lebensraum*. Their 'revisionism' was directed first of all against Poland, simply because Poland was their immediate neighbour to the east; and beyond Poland they looked even further to the east.

Bleak as the situation looked should Germany attack and the Western Allies declare war in support of Poland, the prospects if they failed to do so would be far worse. Besides, the Poles entertained some hope that full support from Britain and France might suffice to deter Hitler from attack, for presumably he did not desire war for its own sake. There can be no doubt today that Hitler would have attacked when the Poles refused his demands, whether or not Poland was linked to the Western Allies. This view receives some oblique confirmation from the actual circumstances of the attack, the nominal German *casus belli*. Reinhard Heydrich staged a 'Polish attack' on the radio station in Gliwice, using prisoners from the concentration camp at Sachsenhausen in Polish uniforms. Not even the excuse for the German attack, still less the real reason, was anything the Poles had done.

We must finally consider the fourth option open to the Poles, the one which was actually chosen: rejecting Hitler's demands and accepting the British guarantee. That guarantee was issued at the end of March 1939, and on 25 August it was replaced by a bilateral Anglo-Polish treaty. The treaty determined mutual assistance against any act of aggression or any threat – direct or indirect – to the independence of the signatories. France had a much older treaty with Poland, with somewhat different provisions; but on 5 September – nearly a week after Hitler's attack – this was replaced by a treaty on similar terms to the British one.

It is now known that just a few hours before the Anglo-Polish treaty was signed, Hitler had issued orders to attack Poland the following morning. In actual fact, that attack was made seven days later, on 1 September. Whatever else the treaty with Britain did, it certainly made the *Führer* pause for a week; so he evidently regarded it as an important factor in the situation.

When we ask ourselves whether the Polish Government was really justified in accepting the British guarantee and invoking aid from the Western Allies, however, we need to consider other factors besides the apparent effect of diplomatic instruments. In particular, it is necessary to understand what was known in Poland about Britain and France.

Poland was linked to France by a friendship centuries old, born out of political co-operation and cultural influence. Napoleon had briefly restored a semi-independent Polish state after the Partitions, and this conjured up warm memories, dear to Polish hearts. When partitioning returned after the defeat of Napoleon, Polish soldiers and underground activists, on the run from Russian or German police, headed for France. For many Poles, France was a second homeland. The French heroic resistance in the First World War was admired in Poland, and association with France seemed to provide the best guarantee that Hitler would be stopped. The Poles trusted France and believed that French promises would be kept.

Great Britain was less well known in Poland than was France, for the two countries shared little of a political or cultural past; but Poles were in general convinced that Britain was the greatest power in the world; that she was a country which did not lose wars, and which honoured her agreements and obligations. Nobody in Poland could have expected that the war would have ended as it did, and that Britain would endorse Russia's formal acquisition of eastern Poland and her political domination of the whole country.

Nor did anybody in Poland believe that the *Blitzkrieg*, forecast by Hitler, was possible, particularly against the West. It was expected that after the Germans attacked Poland, a Franco-British offensive would follow, and that the Germans would find themselves at war on two fronts. The strategic plan of the Polish General Staff was to establish a line of defence in south-east

Poland, against the background of the friendly countries Hungary and Romania. This would hold up the Germans long enough for a great offensive to be built up in the West.

That plan had one extremely weak point: it was not foreseen that Soviet Russia might attack Poland from the east. The Poles should have anticipated this; but it was considered that the ideological differences between Communism and Nazism were so great that Russia would never come to an agreement with Hitler. It was only on 23 August, when the Ribbentrop–Molotov pact was signed, that this was perceived as a possible course of events. It must be remembered, however, that the pact took not only Poland, but the whole world, by surprise. Moreover, it was signed only a week before the invasion and Poland had no chance to change her plans. There was a further imponderable in the situation – whether Britain and France would honour their obligations; but, as we have seen, the Poles had every reason to anticipate that they would.

Today, forty years after, we may reflect that there were factors in the situation – some already known, others still unknown – which might have made Poland pause. There were alarming intelligence reports of the defeatist mood in France which would later prove all too accurate; and there were reports of pacifist attitudes in Britain which would certainly not be corroborated by subsequent experience. We also know now that Hitler's reaction to the British guarantee was not to make his initial attack in the West, but to fall on Poland first of all. Here the Poles may seem to have made a political mistake; for surely everything possible should have been done to delay the German attack and steer Hitler's fury in some other direction.

We now know also of the long-term consequences of Polish resistance. Six million Polish citizens were to perish in the war, and over a million more would be deported to the Soviet Union, where many of them now lie buried. We now know that the Polish state would be forcibly moved to the West, on to former German lands. These lands belonged to Poland many centuries ago and once the Germans started the last war and carried it on in such a brutal way, compensation in the west and north was natural for Poles. Of course, they realised that it would establish a permanent sense of grievance in the minds of the German people. We know, too, that a Communist system would be imposed upon Poland, with Russia in control. Would the Poles still have acted as they did, if they could have foreseen all that?

We must remember another factor, too. Germany had offered promises as well as threats to Poland. At intervals, right from the earliest days of the Nazi regime, unofficial offers had been made to Poland that if she would cede the lands Germany desired and participate in a joint attack on Soviet Russia, then she would be allowed to compensate herself richly in the east. This suggestion was repeated in 1934 by Hermann Göring in his talks with the Polish leader, Marshal Piłsudski; but of course it was rejected. Poland had a peace treaty with Russia, and any aggressive actions against her would have been both suicidal and immoral.

Other kinds of evidence might perhaps be adduced, to suggest that the Polish decision to resist Germany in alliance with Britain and France – whether apparently reasonable or not in the light of evidence available at the time – was in fact wrong. The parallel is sometimes drawn with Hungary. The Hungarians did not merely resist Hitler, they actually fought on his side. As a result they suffered little at his hands; while today their situation is more or less the same as that of the Poles. The parallel, however, is less close than appears to be the case. The Germans never had any 're-visionist' claims against Hungary, and the Hungarian nation did not lie in the way of the German *Drang nach Osten*. In the maniac plans of the Nazis, Hungarians had not been marked down for total destruction, as had been the Jews and, after them, the Poles.

So we return to the question whether, in light of all this subsequent experience, the war might have ended better for Poland if her leaders had made some other decision in 1939. Any other course of behaviour would have resulted in either Germany or Russia securing control of Poland, without the Poles fighting in their own defence. This state of affairs, at the lowest estimate, would have resulted in the Polish people completely losing faith in themselves, and with the victors in the eventual world conflict being under no sort of obligation towards Poland. If we suppose that the upshot of such a war would still have been victory by the 'Big Three' – surely the likeliest hypothesis – then we must recall what Stalin's feelings about Poland were, as revealed at the time of the Nazi–Soviet partitioning in 1939. Hitler wished to annex part of Poland to Germany and was content to allow half of the country to pass to Russia; but he was also prepared to allow a certain part of Poland to remain in existence as a German protectorate – known as the 'General Government'. Stalin wished to go even further than Hitler; for he wanted to obliterate the Polish state entirely, even as a name.

Thanks to her resistance and thanks to her ties with the West, Poland is today on the map of Europe. She is completely within the orbit of Soviet Russia, she is not free politically and her cultural and economic development is severely limited; but she is not one of the Soviet republics, like the Ukraine, Lithuania, Latvia or Estonia.

This conclusion does not mean that the Poles have accepted the political decisions of the Western powers, who agreed to every concession demanded by Stalin. They were not only immoral, but wrong and harmful, they allowed Soviet Russia to gain more than even Stalin himself expected. They created the world order of today, which is a constant threat to the peace, security and freedom of many other countries, not only Poland.

# 6 The Soviet View
**Margot Light**

The Great Patriotic War remains a very real experience to all Russians, whether they are officials, men in the street, or dissidents. Postwar reconstruction has restored most of the devastated areas and the disabled war veterans are less frequently encountered; but the psychological scars remain. There are indelible memories of near-defeat and there is enormous pride in the final victory. There is also deep resentment that the Soviet contribution to this victory is underestimated. The belief that Soviet effort, hardship and sacrifice is not appreciated in the West causes much bitterness, even in people who do not support the regime.

A similar bitterness is prevalent in all Soviet histories of the Second World War. It extends to the accounts of events which led to the outbreak of war in September 1939 and to the policies of all the other belligerents until the German attack on the Soviet Union on 22 June 1941 – and, indeed, throughout the Great Patriotic War.

For Soviet historians, the history of the 1930s is a history of disappointment and betrayal. It is therefore worth considering the Soviet version of 1939 and 1940. Most other aspects of Soviet history have been subject to reconsideration and revision by Soviet writers. There has never been a serious revision of the events of 1939 and 1940. The consistency of the pre-1953, post-1953 and post-1964 versions is astonishing.

I shall give a brief outline of the *Soviet* version of the events which led to the outbreak of war. All Soviet accounts of the interwar period stress the 'peace-loving and peace-pursuing' foreign policy of the Soviet state from the moment of its first foreign policy 'Decree on Peace' until the moment when it had war thrust upon it in 1941. The hostile intentions of the capitalist world became apparent with foreign intervention in the Russian

Civil War and they culminated in the efforts of Britain and France, abetted by the United States, to turn Nazi Germany onto the Soviet Union, in the hope that Fascism and Socialism would mutually annihilate one another – leaving the Western democracies unscathed by war. It is against this background that both the policy of appeasement and the subsequent change in British and French foreign policy are interpreted. From 1934 onwards, the Soviet Union had been attempting to set up a system of collective security in Europe. These efforts were rejected by Britain and France, intent on appeasing Hitler. Soviet historians assure us that 15 March 1939 did not represent a 'revolution' in British foreign policy – as some Western historians claim – the policy which followed the disappearance of Czechoslovakia was merely the old policy of appeasement conducted by other means.[2]

The Soviet response to the demise of Czechoslovakia was to suggest a six-power conference to decide on collective measures to prevent further aggression in Europe. The French ignored the invitation. Chamberlain and Halifax called it 'premature' and said there was no-one senior enough available to attend. When the British ambassador to Moscow enquired what the Soviet Union would do if Romania was attacked, the Russians turned the question back – what would Britain do? The British proposed a four-power declaration of intention to consult in case of aggression. Although the Soviet Government doubted the efficacy of mere *announcements of intentions*, they agreed. But by 1 April the British had dropped the subject of a four-power declaration and had given a unilateral guarantee to Poland. The Russians believe that Britain never intended to honour this guarantee. The Soviet Union was invited to proclaim a similar unilateral guarantee to Poland and Romania, to be operative only if those countries requested aid. The Soviet Government found this proposal unequal, unreciprocal, ineffectual and unacceptable. They counter-proposed a tripartite pact with an explicit military convention. This suggestion was ignored at first, and it was only at the end of May that the British Government began to consider it. But by this time Soviet proposals had become more elaborate: the tripartite pact should guarantee the signatories as well as Belgium, Greece, Turkey, Romania, Poland, Latvia, Estonia and Finland. There was to be no separate peace. A political agreement should be accompanied by a simultaneous military pact. The British and French response to these proposals caused the

Soviet Government to believe that while Britain and France expected aid from the Soviet Union, they were reluctant to reciprocate. The French Government seemed marginally more reasonable, but it was completely dominated by the British. Nevertheless, the Soviet Government invited the British Foreign Secretary, Viscount Halifax, to Moscow for face-to-face negotiations. Halifax declined, and the negotiations were conducted by the ambassador, aided by Strang, a Foreign Office official, on the British side, and Foreign Minister Molotov on the Soviet side.[3]

The talks began on 15 June and proceeded very slowly because of a series of disagreements: Which countries were to be guaranteed? Were they to be guaranteed against both direct and indirect aggression? How was indirect aggression to be defined? Would the political and military agreements come into force simultaneously? A compromise was eventually reached on the list of countries to be guaranteed. On 21 July, before a mutually acceptable definition of indirect aggression had been reached, military talks began. Indirect aggression was destined never to be defined. The military talks ground to a halt, then broke down.[4] It became clear later that Britain was secretly negotiating with Germany at the same time. Soviet historians believe that the British and French hoped that their negotiations with the Soviet Union would put pressure on Hitler to conclude an anti-Soviet agreement with them.[5]

The composition of the military delegations bears witness to the low priority given by Britain and France to an agreement with the Soviet Union. Both countries sent low-ranking officers, who had instructions to delay the talks and keep to general topics. The head of the British delegation, Admiral Drax, had no authority to sign an agreement. The delegations travelled to Moscow by the slowest possible means of transport. The Soviet delegation, headed by Minister of Defence Voroshilov, was empowered to sign an agreement, and had concrete plans for military co-operation in case of each of three directions of attack by Germany. The British and French delegations offered, in return, only platitudes and vague generalisations.[6]

Soviet participation in war against Germany depended, necessarily, on Soviet troops crossing Poland and Romania. So when it turned out that no agreement had been obtained for Soviet troops to cross these countries, the Soviet officials were justifiably sceptical about British and French intentions. The military talks were suspended until Polish and Romanian co-operation had been solicited. Published British documents and Cabinet and Foreign Policy Committee papers establish that the British knew that this permission was essential to the success both of the talks and of the guarantee to Poland. But nothing had been done to persuade the Poles, and nothing was done to persuade them now. Poland refused permission and Romania was never approached. The military talks remained in suspension and Soviet anxiety grew. The Soviet Union was, at that time, fighting Japan in Mongolia. Isolation in a two-front war against Japan in the East and Germany in the West, without a single ally, had to be avoided.

Meanwhile, at the end of May, the German Government had begun to make approaches to the Soviet Government, trying to dissuade it from participating in an 'encirclement' of Germany. The Soviet Chargé d'Affaires in Berlin at first replied that the Soviet Union would not repudiate collective security. German overtures grew more insistent. When it became apparent that an agreement with Britain and France was unlikely, the Soviet leaders agreed that Ribbentrop should visit Moscow. Although they realised that war with Germany was inevitable, even a temporary postponement of that war would enable the Soviet Union to build up its defences. Ribbentrop arrived on 23 August. On that day it became clear that Britain and France had not obtained permission for Soviet troops to cross Polish territory; and so the Soviet Union had no alternative but to sign a non-aggression pact with Germany.[7]

In no official Soviet account of this pact are details given of the secret protocols.[8] The Anglo-Soviet-French talks were broken off. On 1 September Germany invaded Poland. On 3 September, after delay and hesitation, Britain and France declared war on Germany.

Soviet historians believe that even at this stage, the British and French leaders had not yet abandoned hope of appeasing Hitler. They interpret the phoney war as a continuation of the Munich policy of appeasement: the sacrifice of Poland in order to avert war. Military activity in the West was delayed, they believe, in the hope that Hitler would use his freedom of manoeuvre in Poland to move against the Soviet Union.[9] Further evidence that Britain and France had aggressive intentions against the Soviet Union is deduced from the unreasonable response of the Finnish

Government to Soviet attempts to strengthen the defences of Leningrad and the north-western border of the Soviet Union. The Soviet Government proposed exchanging Finnish territory for Soviet territory, so as to move the border further away from Leningrad. Under British and French influence the Finnish Government broke off negotiations, and Finnish military provocations caused war to break out on 30 November 1939. Instead of fighting Germany, France and Britain immediately sent arms to Finland, and Britain prepared to send an emergency expeditionary force to take part in the war against the Soviet Union. Finland signed a peace treaty with the Soviet Union in March 1940 despite British, French and American objections. Although the Soviet Union achieved its desired territorial changes, Finland gradually got drawn further and further into the orbit of Nazi Germany, and continued to pose a threat to the Soviet Union.[10]

Much alarmed by Germany's rapid defeat of Poland, which brought German forces closer and closer to the Soviet border, the Soviet Government undertook defensive diplomatic and military action. Soviet troops crossed the Polish border on 17 September. By 25 September the Soviet army had saved twelve million Western Ukrainians and Western Byelorussians from the threat of Fascist enslavement, and had reunited them with the rest of the Ukraine and Byelorussia, from whom they had been separated since 1920. The border of the Soviet Union was moved 250–350 km westwards. On 28 September a Soviet–German border agreement was signed, recognising the new western border of the Soviet Union as approximating the old Curzon line.[11]

There remained a risk that the Baltic states would be used to launch an attack on the Soviet Union. Public pressure forced the Governments of Estonia, Latvia and Lithuania to sign mutual aid pacts with the Soviet Union. The Soviet Union was granted the right to construct bases and to station troops in these countries. Hostile forces within the Baltic republics began to sabotage Soviet forces and to prepare for war against the Soviet Union. Moreover, there was a danger that these countries would soon be included in the German Reich. This incensed the populace and led to uprisings. Popular democratic governments took power in Lithuania, Latvia and Estonia in June 1940. After elections in July, the Supreme Soviet was requested to grant admission of these countries into the Soviet Union. This development vastly improved the defences of the Soviet Union.[12]

The Soviet Government was also concerned about the security of its south-western borders. Many of the Balkan states were actively co-operating with Germany. Relations between Romania and the Soviet Union were particularly strained because Romania refused to give back Bessarabia, seized in 1918, or to settle the problem of Northern Bukovina, whose population wanted to join with the Ukraine. Romanian approaches to Germany for aid against the Soviet Union were refused: Germany was not yet ready to attack the Soviet Union. Romania was forced to give way, and in August 1940 Bessarabia was united with Soviet Moldavia and Northern Bukovina was joined to the Ukraine. This astute political move by the Soviet Government increased the security of the south-western border and moved it 200 km to the west. Soviet fears about Romania proved well grounded, when Romania joined the Axis at the end of 1940.[13]

Throughout 1940, and on until June 1941, the Soviet Union scrupulously observed the terms of the Soviet–German Non-Aggression Pact, and fulfilled its obligations under the economic agreements between the two countries. In April 1941 it persuaded the Japanese to sign a neutrality pact, thereby ensuring the Soviet eastern border. The alarming prospect of a two-front war when Germany finally turned on the Soviet Union faded. Although the timing of Germany's inevitable attack was miscalculated, intensive preparations were made to increase Soviet military potential and strengthen Soviet defences. Efforts were made to reassure Germany about Soviet peaceful intentions and to delay the outbreak of war.[14] In spite of these efforts, and without a formal declaration, Germany attacked the Soviet Union on 22 June 1941. The Second World War, until that moment an unjust imperialist war, became a just war of liberation eventually fought by an anti-fascist coalition of the greatest states in the world, the Soviet Union, the United States and Britain.[15]

That, in all-too-brief summary, is how Soviet historians tell the story. They lay particular stress on the sincerity of the Soviet leaders' intention to reach an agreement with Britain and France, their belief that such an agreement would have prevented German aggression, and their conviction that an effective agreement *had* to be accompanied by a military pact. There is a strong sense of outrage that Britain and France intended to bind the Soviet Union by an unequal treaty which would guarantee Soviet aid for the West, without reciprocal action from the West

in case of a German attack on the Soviet Union. Since there was
no common Soviet–German border, it is self-evident to Soviet
historians that any German attack would be preceded by an
attack on one of the Eastern European states bordering the Soviet
Union. Common sense, then, dictated that any pact which did
not guarantee these states would be useless. But these states had a
long history of animosity towards the Soviet Union. Moreover,
Germany had produced, in Austria and in Czechoslovakia,
examples of effective 'indirect aggression'. Therefore any
guarantee of the states bordering on the Soviet Union also had to
subsume the possibility that one of these states might voluntarily,
or under non-violent coercion, join with Germany in an attack on
the Soviet Union. This imposed the necessity for a guarantee even
in cases of indirect aggression.

British protests that no state which did not want a Soviet
guarantee could be included in the pact, since this would infringe
the sovereignty of that state, is pure hypocrisy, in the view of
Soviet historians – and they point to the blatant infringement of
Czech sovereignty at Munich to support their view.[16] Geography
dictated that the Soviet army could only engage with the German
army in support of France and Britain if it could reach Germany
via either Poland or Romania, or both. The failure of Britain and
France to tie their guarantee of these countries to this condition,
and to get permission from Poland and Romania prior to the
military talks, is further proof that neither Britain nor France
were ever serious about the tripartite pact. Conclusive evidence
for this lack of seriousness is adduced from the slow British
response to Soviet suggestions and proposals and the length of
time the negotiations took. Insult was added to injury when
Strang, head of the Central Department of the Foreign Office,
was sent without any power to sign an agreement to aid the
British ambassador in the political negotiations. After all, it had
been Chamberlain himself who had visited Hitler.[17] This sense of
insult was increased when the membership of the military
missions became known. Most accounts mention that the leader
of the British delegation, Admiral Drax, was in semi-retirement
and had a reputation for being anti-Soviet, and that General
Doumenc was a 'nonentity'.[18]

To Soviet scholars these facts indicate that Britain and France
lacked both seriousness and a sense of urgency in their negotiations with the Soviet Union. Given the alarming international

situation, the negotiations must have had some aim other than
that of concluding a pact. And there is unanimous agreement
that the aim can only have been to put pressure on Hitler. To
prevent a tripartite pact and a war on two fronts, Hitler would
return to a Munich-type policy, come to an agreement with the
Western powers and move eastwards for his *Lebensraum*. The
fact that it was with the Soviet Union that Hitler made his pact is
a tribute to Soviet diplomatic acumen – in a flash the perfidious
plans of British and French imperialism were ruined, the Soviet
Union was saved from the prospect of a two-front war without
allies, and time was gained for perfecting the means with which
to wage the war that must ultimately come.

Furthermore, the acquistion of areas lost in 1918–20 not only
satisfied irredentist claims, but also provided insurance for Soviet
territorial integrity in the future battles. The Soviet Union, in
pursuing its national interest, and accepting the only option
available – a non-aggression pact with Germany – was also
fulfilling its international duty. The future of the international
Communist movement depended on a strong, viable and
impregnable Soviet Union.[19]

The most remarkable thing about the Soviet version of the
events I have been relating is the consistency with which this view
of history has been maintained over the years. In vain does one
look for a scholarly debate in Soviet history books, for newly discovered facts and new interpretations. Insofar as there is a debate
at all, it is a debate with the Western revisionist school. Those
historians who justify appeasement are criticised as severely as
those who blame the Soviet Union for the outbreak of the war.
They are 'bourgeois falsificators' of history, intent on white-
washing British, French and American conduct in the prewar
years. The American publication, in 1948, of documents on
Nazi–Soviet relations was interpreted as a blow in the Cold War.[20]
Soviet historians have continued fighting this Cold War in thirty
years of published accounts of the history of the prewar period
and the early months of the war. Contemporary accounts use, for
their sources, not new Soviet archival material, but published
Soviet sources, archive material referred to in older books (most
of it from captured enemy archives) and Western sources. Since
the opening of the British archives, more and more frequent
reference is made to Cabinet papers and Foreign Office
materials. Soviet historians find new evidence in these papers of

British perfidy during the Anglo-Soviet-French negotiations, and they find confirmation of their view that the British wanted to direct the Nazis eastward.

The process of de-Stalinisation had some effect on the writing of history in general but, as already noted, made very little impact on the treatment of the 1939–41 period. If war history served the cult of the leader before 1953, since 1953 it has served the cult of the party, and it has been used to legitimise the rule of the new leaders.[21] Even when, for a few years, it became fashionable to criticise Stalin, little leeway was given to diplomatic and military historians. In 1965 Aleksandr Nekrich published *22 June 1941*, in which the defeat suffered by the Soviet army at the start of the war was attributed to Stalin, his purge of the army in 1937, his lack of leadership, his refusal to believe reports of an imminent attack, and the retarded state of military and defence preparations. Although this book was widely praised at the time of publication, within two years it had been severely criticised, withdrawn from circulation and its author vilified.[22] Nekrich has since left the Soviet Union. Most histories written since refer to the 'miscalculations' about when the German attack would take place and the resulting incomplete state of Soviet defences. Nowhere is this analysed or even described in detail. Very seldom is the effect of the purges even mentioned in official histories. Memoirists are rather bolder in this repect. Khrushchev blames both Stalin and Voroshilov for the fact that the best Soviet commanders had been eliminated, and for the shortage of armaments.[23] Zhukov mentions that poor leadership in the army was the aftermath of mass promotion to high ranks of young officers after the unjustified arrest of prominent military leaders.[24] In other memoirs one finds vivid descriptions of the chaos which reigned in the military from 1937 onwards and after the outbreak of war.[25]

The publicity accorded to Soviet dissidents in the West often makes it seem that they are numerous. In fact there are very few, and few of those few are historians. And those few dissident historians are severely handicapped by lack of access to primary sources, and often even to foreign secondary sources. It is interesting, for example, to note that Liddell Hart's history of the Second World War was translated a couple of years ago in an edited version which omitted all unfavourable references to the Soviet Union.[26]

In vain, then, does one look for a coherent and detailed dissident version of the events of 1939 and 1940. Roy Medvedev justifies the signing of the Ribbentrop–Molotov pact (and many Western historians would agree with him); but he criticises the secret protocols and claims that Stalin misjudged the pact's domestic implications. The terms of the protocols to the boundary agreement of 29 September resulted in a halt to anti-fascist propaganda in the Soviet Union, and this psychologically disarmed Soviet citizens.[27] Furthermore, he admits that when the Soviet Union took over the Baltic republics, the Western Ukraine and Western Byelorussia, thousands of completely innocent people were repressed and there was mass deportation of local people eastwards.[28]

Major General Grigorenko is harsher in his judgements. In a spirited defence of Nekrich's *22 June*, he points out that the losses in the Soviet High Command during the purges were greater than the losses suffered by the German and Japanese High Commands during the war.[29] He also claims that although the Nazi–Soviet pact is usually justified because of the time gained by the Soviet Union, this time was so badly used that the Soviet Union was even less prepared for war in 1941 than it had been in 1939. The old fortified borders had been destroyed before new fortified areas had been completed, reserve supplies were concentrated in areas near the new borders, new airfields were in the process of being constructed but had not been completed. The Soviet air force on civilian airfields was a sitting target for the German air force. New mechanised forces were in the process of being formed but were incomplete and untrained. Effective anti-tank guns had been taken out of production and the army was not in a state of military alert.[30] 'Why was it', Grigorenko asks, 'that our country which had for so long been preparing for the certain attack of the combined forces of world imperialism, in fact for the first six months could not withstand the attack of the German army alone supported only by part of the forces of three German satellites?'[31]

Insofar as there is a revisionist or dissident history of the war, then, it concentrates on the effect of the purges, on the inadequacy of Stalin and Voroshilov's military preparations and planning, and the military disasters which occurred from 22 June 1941 until the battle of Stalingrad. No Soviet historian, dissident or official, criticises Stalin for signing the non-aggression pact, or finds fault with any aspect of Soviet diplomacy other than the 'ideological disarming' that followed the pact.

This 'ideological disarming' had an impact which extended beyond the borders of the Soviet Union. While there is little doubt that the Nazi–Soviet non-aggression pact served the Soviet national interest, the Soviet claim that it also satisfied the interests of the international Communist movement is hardly credible. Members of the Comintern were instructed to support the pact, and to cease anti-Fascist activity and propaganda. This caused consternation within the movement and had serious repercussions on European Communist parties.[32] There was an exodus from the parties themselves, and the Communist image became badly tarnished. Whether we consider the pact itself as reasonable or not, the insistence that the Comintern disarm itself was unreasonable, unnecessary and harmful. By the end of the war, Soviet victory, German repression of Communists, and Communist activity in resistance movements had gone some way towards restoring the prestige of the movement. But there were and are ex-Party members and Marxists who remember with bitterness and shame the embarrassment of the volte-face forced upon them. And it is a fact that the Soviet Government had, in its relations with other governments, steadfastly denied responsibility for Comintern activity throughout the 1920s and 1930s, and then in August 1939 it suddenly declared that the success of the Nazi–Soviet pact would be dependent upon European Communists following the Moscow line and withdrawing their support from anti-Fascist movements.

Soviet official histories omit any analysis of the real effects of the Nazi–Soviet pact on the international Communist movement. Could it be that the strident tilting at windmills, the constant justification of the Molotov–Ribbentrop pact, is meant to blot out any suspicion that the Soviet Union might, in 1939, have given priority to national interest, over and above international interest and ideological consistency?

Finally, how does the Soviet account differ from Western accounts? Although Western accounts interpret the Soviet take-over of the Baltic republics and Bessarabia as a less humane gesture, and find other explanations for the phoney war, many of the facts mentioned by Soviet historians are substantiated and echoed in Western sources. Since 1970, Soviet historians have made skilful use of the archive material available in the West. There have been few disclosures based on newly accessible Soviet archive materials. If Western histories of 1939 and 1940, and Soviet histories of the same period are based on the same set of facts and documents, why does one experience what almost amounts to culture shock on reading the Soviet version?

It is, I suppose, partly a question of tone. The solemnity with which each and every Soviet historian approaches his topic cannot be aspired to by even the most official of British historians. Striking too, is the absence of hypotheses, alternative explanations, doubts and uncertainties. Not only is there no reported gossip from the Soviet corridors of power – there is no mention of any dialogue or discussion within the Soviet leadership, no hint of a decision-making process. One must assume that Stalin asked advice from his closest collaborators. But Khrushchev, a member of the Politburo at the time, claims to have heard about Ribbentrop's visit to Moscow only on the day prior to his arrival, and he says in his memoirs: 'I was . . . part of Stalin's ruling circle, but I still had no way of knowing that we were woefully lacking in rifles, and machine guns, not to mention tanks and heavy artillery'.[33] Khrushchev might be an unreliable witness, who had good reasons for attempting to dissociate himself from Stalin's leadership. But there is nowhere a hint of consultation, detail of deliberation, accounts of conversations amongst the Soviet leaders themselves, rather than exchanges between individual Soviet leaders, and leaders of other countries. In the official histories it is always the impersonal, united voice of the Soviet leadership which decides and then acts.[34]

Dissension and discussion are credited to French, British, even the German Governments, but no allowance is made for vacillation, stupidity, incompetence or uncertainty on their part. Those Governments act within a conspiracy framework, following a grand design of imperialism predestined to oppose socialism and to work for its destruction.

Perhaps it is the Soviet Marxist theory of history and of historical scholarship that makes this tone, this single interpretation and monolithic view, inevitable. It is believed that history develops according to material laws and can therefore be studied scientifically. Once the facts have been discovered, Marxist historians must 'establish [their] class character'.[35] This will establish objective social laws. Once a historical situation has been understood objectively, no re-interpretation should be necessary, or indeed possible. Moreover, history and historical science have to serve not only genuine enquiry: they should expose 'bourgeois falsifiers of the . . . history of the USSR in the Second World War'.[36] Furthermore, scholars of history have political and educational duties to perform: 'History is also called upon to educate the people, and in particular our youth, in the revolutionary, patriotic and work traditions, in the heroic deeds of earlier generations'.[37] Nowhere, except perhaps in the history of the revolution itself, is this duty felt more strongly, more poignantly, than in the history of the Great Patriotic War.

## NOTES AND REFERENCES

1. For a pre-1953 version see 'Falsifiers of History', supplement to *New Times*, no. 8, 18 February 1948; for the post-1953 version see P. N. Pospelov *et al.* (eds), *Istoriya Velikoi Otechestvennoi voiny Sovetskogo Soyuza* (*History of the Great Patriotic War of the Soviet Union*), vol. 1 (Moscow, 1961); and for a more recent account, see A. A. Grechko *et al.* (eds), *Istoriya vtoroi mirovoi voiny* (*History of the Second World War*), vols 2 and 3 (Moscow, 1974).

2. Grechko *et al. Istoriya vtoroi mirovoi voiny* vol. 2, p. 126.

3. For a detailed Soviet account of events preceding the face-to-face negotiations, see A. A. Gromyko *et al.* (eds), *Istoriya diplomatii* (*Diplomatic History*) 2nd edn, vol. 3 (Moscow, 1965) pp. 769−78.

4. A description of the negotiations can be found in ibid., pp. 778−95. Documentary records of the talks were published by the USSR Ministry of Foreign Affairs in 1948 (*Documents and Materials Relating to the Eve of the Second World War*) (Moscow, 1948). The records of the military negotiations were republished in *International Affairs* (Moscow) nos 2 and 3, February and March 1959, and were included in A. A. Gromyko *et al.* (eds), *SSSR v bor'be za mir nakanune vtoroi mirovoi voiny* (*USSR in the Struggle for Peace on the Eve of the Second World War*) (Moscow, 1971).

5. See, for example, V. M. Khvostov 'Anglo-germanskie peregovory 1939 goda', (*Anglo-German Negotiations, 1939*), *Izvestiya*, 7 July 1948, reprinted in V. M. Khvostov, *Problemy istorii vneshnei politiki SSSR i mezhdunarodnykh otnoshenii* (*Problems of the history of the foreign policy of USSR and of International Relations*). (Moscow, 1976) pp. 56−61; and A. M. Nekrich (ed.), *Protiv falsifikatsii istorii vtoroi mirovoi voiny* (*Against the Falsification of the History of the Second World War*) (Moscow, 1964) pp. 151 and 181.

6. The composition and instructions of the British and French military missions are criticised in all Soviet sources, including relevant memoirs. See, for example, Marshal G. K. Zhukov, *The Memoirs of Marshal Zhukov* (London, 1971) p. 176.

7. For an account of the German−Soviet negotiations, see Gromyko *et al.* (eds), *Istoriya diplomatii*, vol. 3, pp. 796−8.

8. The full text of the Nazi–Soviet Non-Aggression Pact and the secret protocols was published in R. J. Sontag and J. S. Beddie (eds), *Nazi–Soviet Relations 1939–1945: Documents from the Archives of the German Foreign Office* (Washington DC, 1948). This book aroused an immediate wrathful response, see 'Falsifiers of History'. Oblique reference to the secret protocols is made in I. M. Maisky, *Who Helped Hitler?* (London, 1964) p. 201, and in N. S. Khrushchev, *Khrushchev Remembers* (London, 1971) p. 121.

9. The interpretation of the phoney war as a betrayal of Poland and an attempt to turn Germany on the USSR is not limited to accounts written during the Cold War. It can also be found in Nekrich (ed.) *Protiv falsifikatsii istorii*, p. 236, and in Grechko *et al.* (eds), *Istoriya vtoroi mirovoi voiny*, vol. 3, p. 27. Vol. 4 of Gromyko *et al.* (eds), *Istoriya diplomatii*, deals with the outbreak of the war, and makes the same claim (pp. 7–9). The second edition of this volume appeared in 1975. See also the standard, official foreign policy textbook, A. A. Gromyko and B. N. Ponomarev (eds), *Istoriya vneshnei politiki SSSR 1917–1945*. (*The History of the Foreign Policy of the USSR*), vol. 1 (Moscow, 1976) pp. 395–9.

10. An account of the abortive Soviet–Finnish talks is given in Grechko *et al.* (eds), *Istoriya vtoroi mirovoi voiny*, vol. 3, pp. 358–65. Initial Soviet defeats in the war against Finland are attributed to insufficient preparedness. See also Gromyko and Ponomarev (eds), *Istoriya vneshnei politiki SSSR*, pp. 406–11.

11. Both Gromyko *et al.* (eds), *Istoriya diplomatii*, vol. 4, p. 20, and Grechko *et al.* (eds) *Istoriya vtoroi mirovoi voiny* vol. 3, pp. 355–7 describe the liberation of Western Ukraine and Western Byelorussia. It is also defined as a measure to save the inhabitants from Fascist enslavement by Nekrich, in the book which was later to cause so much furore: A. M. Nekrich *22 I'unya, 1941* (Moscow, 1965). For a personal account of the invasion, see Marshal A. L. Eremenko *V nachale voiny* (*At the Beginning of the War*) (Moscow, 1965) ch. 1.

12. All Soviet sources stress that popular pressure forced the governments of the Baltic states to sign the mutual aid pacts and then led to the inclusion of these states in the USSR. See, for example, Nekrich (ed.) *Protiv falsifikatsii istorii* and *22 I'unya, 1941*. Identical explanations are to be found in A. A. Grechko (ed.), *Liberation Mission of the Soviet Armed Forces in the Second World War* (Moscow, 1975) pp. 28–9; and in A. L. Narochnitskii *et al.* (eds), *60 let bor'by za mir i bezopasnost'* (*60 years of the Struggle of the USSR for Peace and Security)* (Moscow, 1979) pp. 136–40. The strategic importance to the USSR of the Baltic republics is mentioned by Khrushchev in *Krushchev Remembers*, pp. 131–2.

13. Soviet sources fail to mention the adverse affect of this move against Romania on Soviet–German relations, and Hitler's decision to attack the Soviet Union. See, for example, Grechko, *et al.* (eds), *Istoriya vtoroi mirovoi voiny*, vol. 3, pp. 369–71; Gromyko and Ponomarev (eds), *Istoriya vneshnei politiki SSSR*, pp. 411–12; and Narochnitskii *et al.* (eds) *60 let bor'by za mir i bezopasnost'*, pp. 140–4.

14. Soviet relations with Germany during the period of the non-aggression pact are referred to only briefly in Soviet histories of this period. Soviet authors themselves lament the almost exclusive concentration on the Anglo-French-Soviet talks. See, for example, A. D. Chikvaidze, *Angliskii Kabinet*

*nakanune vtoroi mirovoi voiny* (*The English Cabinet on the Eve of the Second World War*). (Tbilisi, 1976) p. 29. In the introduction to S. Bialer (ed.) *Stalin and His Generals: Soviet Military Memoirs of World War II* (London, 1970), Bialer points out that most of the original documents published in Soviet journals are either captured German documents or reprints from British and American sources. Soviet documents appear to be out of reach even to Soviet scholars.

15. For definitions of the nature of the war, see Grechko, *et al.* (eds), *Istoriya vtoroi mirovoi voiny*, vol. 3, p. 444; and P. A. Zhilin, *The Second World War and Our Time*. (Moscow, 1978) p. 105.

16. The accusation of hypocrisy is made particularly forcefully in Chikvaidze, *Angliskii Kabinet*, p. 170. This study makes extensive use of British Cabinet papers and other archive material.

17. Ibid., pp. 196–7. For a personal account of the frustration experienced in trying to get the British to negotiate, see Maisky, *Who Helped Hitler?*. For the disrespect implied by Strang's rank, see Zhilin, *The Second World War*, pp. 13–14.

18. See V. Ya. Sipols, *Sovetskii Soyuz v bor'be za mir i bezopasnost', 1933–39* (*The Soviet Union in the Struggle for Peace and Security 1933–39*) (Moscow, 1974) pp. 353–4; Gromyko *et al.* (eds) *Istoriya diplomatii*, vol. 3, p. 789 and Gromyko and Ponomarev (eds), *Istoriya vneshnei politiki SSSR*, p. 373 for examples.

19. For the positive international implications of the non-aggression pact, see Nekrich, *Protiv falsifikatsii istorii*, p. 200; and Khvostov, *Problemy istorii vneshnei politiki SSSR*, p. 412. For a dissenting opinion of its effect on the international communist movement, see Fernando Claudin, *The Communist Movement* (Harmondsworth, 1975) ch. 4.

20. Sontag and Beddie (eds), *Nazi–Soviet Relations 1939–1945*.

21. Bialer (ed.), *Stalin and His Generals*, pp. 17–19.

22. For an English translation of this book, and an account of the controversy it produced, see Vladimir Petrov, *'22 June 1941': Soviet Historians and the German Invasion* (Columbia, 1968).

23. Khrushchev, *Krushchev Remembers*, pp. 141–6.

24. Zhukov, *The Memoirs of Marshal Zhukov*, p. 183.

25. See Bialer (ed.), *Stalin and His Generals*, for a selection of translated extracts from military memoirs.

26. For a review of the Russian translation and a comparison with the original, see B. E. Lewis, 'Soviet Taboo', *Soviet Studies*, XXIX, 4 (October 1977), pp. 603–6.

27. Roy A. Medvedev, *K sudu istorii* (*Let History Judge*) (New York, 1974) pp. 872–5. The English translation of this book (*Let History Judge*, London, 1971) is an abridged version, and it omits Medvedev's comments on the secret protocols.

28. Ibid., pp. 477–8.

29. Pyotr Grigor'evich Grigorenko, *Mysli sumashedshego* (*Thoughts of a Madman*) (Amsterdam, 1973) p. 82.

30. Ibid., pp. 80–1.

31. Ibid., p. 45.

32. Medvedev, *K sudu istorii*, pp. 875–7. See also Claudin, *The Communist Movement*, p. 295.

33. Khrushchev, *Krushchev Remembers*, p. 142.
34. The Russian language aids this kind of impersonal reporting. There is a special 'indefinite-personal' construction which does not have a specific subject doing a particular action. The action is done passively, or by an unspecified 'them'.
35. Zhilin, *The Second World War*, p. 122.
36. Ibid., p. 123.
37. Khvostov, *Problemy istorii vneshnei politiki SSSR*, p. 380.

# 7 Reflections

**Roy Douglas**

Whatever else emerges from these chapters, they certainly throw some useful light on one of the most vexing problems of twentieth-century history. Granted that Britain, France, Poland and Russia were together a great deal stronger than Germany; granted that all of them perceived fearful dangers to themselves from German expansion; why was it that these four countries failed to link together in an alliance which would probably have stopped Germany without war? The contributors have highlighted the fundamental differences which underlay their apparent community of interest.

The same objective facts took on very different aspects according to the vantage-point from which they were viewed. A. J. P. Taylor discussed – in his characteristic and challenging manner – whether one is even entitled to speak of such a thing as a 'British view'. No doubt similar reservations might be entered about every other country's 'view'. In whatever limited sense it may be legitimate to talk about national 'views', the 'British view' was certainly something very different from the 'view' of the French, the Poles and the Russians in 1939, and those three views were no less different from each other. One fact on which Hitler relied in most of his international transactions was that the 'views' of countries which apparently had common interests in restraining him would prove sufficiently diverse in practice for him to be able to drive wedges between those countries.

In spite of all reservations, it is sometimes convenient to think of matters as if the Polish, Russian, French and British Governments were really free agents, epitomising the collective wills of their countries in dealing with the situation confronting them in 1939. Looking not so much at the military future of a possible alliance, but rather at the situation within each particular country: what motivated those countries to take the decisions they did; and were those decisions wise? It is necessary to define our date of reference – perhaps the most convenient point is the immediate aftermath of the German seizure of Prague on 15 March 1939.

Józef Garliński analyses this problem at considerable depth in respect of Poland, and it is not necessary to recapitulate his points. Suffice to say that he appears to have produced a very compelling argument for the view that the Polish Government probably had no alternative to the course which it took; while if it did have any choice, the course taken was almost certainly the wisest of the appalling options available.

Over the past forty years, many people have said that Polish diplomacy was tortuous. The country's problems have been analysed by Anna Cienciala[1] and one thing is quite clear: the Poles, who had a surfeit of 'minority problems' already, did not wish to acquire any more territory to the east or west. World reactions, and even internal Polish reactions, to their foolish action over Teschen in October 1938, certainly did not whet the appetite for further adventures on a grander scale. Yet the Poles had deep suspicions that the Germans, or Russians, or both of them, had designs on Poland; and Polish policy was over-whelmingly concerned to avoid any inclination towards one of the two great neighbours which could possibly be construed by the other as 'ganging up', and might therefore provoke an attack. There was the further suspicion that an attack on Poland from either of them would produce a counter-invasion from the other: whether ostensibly in Poland's defence, or as an act of concerted aggression. Thus Poland was always bound to avoid giving un-necessary offence to either neighbour; and such a policy necessarily takes on the appearance of duplicity to other countries, whose choices were less difficult.

If Germany invaded Poland, France knew that her obligations towards the Poles would be activated. Douglas Johnson's observa-tion about 'escape clauses' is highly significant; but even if the French could draw upon some legalistic excuse for not going to Poland's aid against a German attack, they were well aware that any course of behaviour which was perceived by others as renegation upon treaties would have grave consequences. It would serve as notice to everybody else in the world – including Britain – that French treaties were worthless. France would cease to signify in the councils of the world, and she would have no friends on whom to call if Germany or anybody else later encroached upon her territory or vital interests.

The position of France in 1939 was almost as agonising as that of Poland, and Britons are not always willing to make fair allowance for France's difficulties. France, unlike Britain, had not won all her remembered wars. Also, unlike Britain, France had a land frontier with Germany and twice within living memory there had been German soldiers on French soil. Far more French soldiers than British had died in the 1914 war. For France as for Poland, the overriding requirement was security; and the quest for security led different people at different times to policies which on their face were wholly contradictory. It was this quest for security which had led France to set up alliances with Czechoslovakia, Poland and Russia; it was the same quest which caused many Frenchmen, from the time of the 1938 crisis onwards, to question the value of those alliances and seek their abrogation. Would France be more secure if she joined with others in saying 'Thus far, but no further' to Germany, or if she allowed Germany a free hand in the East?

There was much to be said for either point of view. Anthony Adamthwaite,[2] shows how Foreign Minister Bonnet could at one moment be contemplating 'revision' of France's Eastern commitments, and a little later could be found encouraging Britain to give her own guarantee to Poland, which had no meaning or value unless France was similarly committed. During the summer of 1939, when negotiations proceeded between Britain and France on one side and Russia on the other, the French were far more willing than the British to make enormous concessions at the expense of Russia's neighbours in order to bring Russia into the same alliance, to block Germany. In the last week of peace, after the Russo-German Non-Aggression Pact had been concluded, differences appeared between those French leaders who wished to stand by Poland and those who desired some sort of mediation – perhaps from Mussolini – in order to preserve peace. The argument for standing by Poland turned on the belief that the Poles could hold Germany long enough to enable large British forces to rally to France's aid; the case for averting war at almost any cost was a re-vamping of the old argument that France would be more secure without her Eastern alliances.

Britain's problems, as revealed in these various studies, were no less remarkable. Traditionally, she had refused to enter commitments to countries which she could not reach by sea. There had been an aberration from that policy over Czechoslovakia in 1938, which had manifestly failed to achieve its primary purpose; so why not revert to the old rule? In the aftermath of the seizure of Prague, this possibility was never advocated as forcefully in Britain as in France. When Ian Colvin's book, *The Chamberlain Cabinet*,[3] was published in 1971, revealing his own role as a 'catalyst' for Government policy at the end of March 1939, it appeared that Britain had been more or less stampeded into her most crucial decision, the guarantee to Poland. Simon Newman's more recent work, *March 1939: the British Guarantee to Poland*,[4] brings out the important fact that the possibility of such a guarantee had been considered for more than a week in the corridors of the Foreign Office before Colvin's interview with Chamberlain and Halifax took place. Yet this does not derogate from the view that his interview proved of crucial importance in crystallising policy, for it led the Prime Minister and the Cabinet to agree to immediate action. Neville Chamberlain's mind is best revealed in a letter to his sister. The young journalist gave the

news . . . that Hitler had everything ready for a swoop on Poland which he planned to split up between annexation and protectorate. This would be followed by the absorption of Lithuania and then other states would be an easy prey. After that would come the possibility of a Russo-German alliance and finally the British Empire, the ultimate goal, would fall helplessly into the German maw.[5]

Confirmatory information was received from another source – 'and the thought that we might wake up on Sunday or Monday morning to find Poland surrendering [?] to an ultimatum was certainly alarming. We then and there decided that we should have to make some such declaration as' the guarantee to Poland[6] – although it was necessary first to refer the matter to the Cabinet.

Yet why that guarantee? Chamberlain's statement that conquest of the British Empire was Hitler's ultimate aim would seem difficult to defend in serious argument. The fact seems to be that emotional considerations completely overrode calculations of advantage in the minds of practically everybody, from the Prime Minister to the man in the street. Matters were seen in terms of

something between *amour propre* and altruism. Hitler had viol-
ated his agreement at Munich and must be 'stopped'. The fact that
Britain did not herself possess the means of 'stopping' him entered
no more into British calculations than similar considerations did
with Poland. Britain had won a great many wars in the past;
nobody was at that moment in a mood to reflect that this war
might be lost, or that the victory might prove Pyrrhic in
character. Even if Chamberlain and his Cabinet had been
determined to avert further commitments, the forces of public
opinion (*pace* A. J. P. Taylor) were too strong to resist. This point
would be illustrated later at that dramatic meeting of the House
of Commons on 2 September 1939, when MPs (reasonably,
though wrongly) suspected that the Government was trying to
duck out of declaring war, and it became plain that the Parliamentary situation could not be held unless an immediate declaration was made.

The question was asked at the time, and it has been asked
repeatedly ever since, why Poland rather than Russia became
Britain's first Eastern ally. The main answer is surely geography:
Poland adjoined Germany, Russia did not. For a brief space
between the seizure of Prague and the Colvin interview, there had
been a possibility that Germany proposed to thrust through
Hungary to Romania; and in that context there would have been
a real choice between the two possible alliances; but if Poland
herself was to be the next target of German expansion, there was
no real choice at all. A British alliance with Russia – against
Poland's wishes, and carrying the threat of a double invasion –
would hardly have deterred Poland from capitulating to German
demands: it would have made it much more likely that the Poles
would capitulate. Chamberlain's object was not to engineer an
alliance which would defeat Germany at the end of a world war –
with scant concern for the fate of countries lying between the
giants. His object was to surround Germany with a ring of allies
who were visibly prepared to fight if any one of them was
attacked, in the desperate hope that such a demonstration would
check Hitler without war. There is little evidence to suggest that
anybody at that moment gave very much thought to the likely
course of war if one did break out despite all efforts: the overriding concern was to try to avert it by the only available means
short of giving Hitler *carte blanche* in the East.

When the guarantee was given, there was still some reason for hoping that the alliance could be extended to include Russia. This would greatly enhance the prospect of deterring Germany without war; while if war came nevertheless then victory would be more likely. Nobody who reads the confidential documents of the period can have the least doubt that the people who mattered in both Britain and France were absolutely sincere in their desire to bring Russia into the alliance; but different people had very different ideas as to the price they were willing to pay in order to do so. Unfortunately, both Russia and Poland had obvious reservations about a four-power alliance.

Any possible Russian participation involved not just one imponderable, but a whole mass of them. In the first place, how effective were the Russians likely to prove in war, even if the Poles could be persuaded to swallow all their reservations? Stalin had just liquidated two-thirds of the Red Army High Command and vast numbers of civilian officials. Western diplomats could get no reliable information about the current strength of the Red Army, for the very good reason that no Russian dared go near their embassies, and diplomatic officials could not move about the country to make their own assessment. Such evidence as the Western powers possessed suggested that the Soviet Union could defend itself against attack, but had no power yet to strike against an external enemy. That view was well corroborated by later experience. Other things being equal, however, there could be no serious doubt that participation of Russia in the alliance would augment its strength substantially, and might well prove of crucial importance in persuading Hitler not to go to war at all.

Yet other things were not equal. What frightened not only the Poles but also some very important people in Britain was the suspicion that Russia had an entirely different view of an alliance from their own. The British, Polish and, indeed, the French, idea of a desirable alliance was something not wildly different from the relationship which had existed between Britain or France on the one hand and Belgium on the other during the 1914 war. No doubt Britain and France fought alongside Belgium for the sake of their own security rather than Belgium's; but they had every intention that Belgium should be restored as fully as possible to its prewar condition once the conflict was over, with all internal and external rights of a sovereign state, and with its territory fully intact. Nobody contemplated, for example, that the Walloon area should be forcibly annexed to France, or that the country should be compelled to accept a government of French stooges, held in office by the French army. By contrast, the Poles of 1939 suspected that Russia's concern was not to secure a base for fighting Germany which she would relinquish when the danger was over, but to find a pretext for annexing eastern Poland at the least, and perhaps for swallowing up the whole country as a Soviet republic. Even if the British believed that this suspicion was ill-founded, they could hardly ignore it. Having just guaranteed Poland against German aggression, Britain could not invite Russia to send her troops into Poland, in full knowledge that the Poles would regard such intervention by Russia as wanton aggression, and probably as an act of war. Perhaps – thus we may cosily reflect from our armchairs today – Britain ought never to have guaranteed Poland in the way that she did; but the fact remained that the guarantee had been given, the Poles had accepted it and thereby incurred Hitler's implacable enmity; and Britain was compelled to act on its implications.

Subsequent discussions showed that Poland had every reason for her suspicions. The Russians demanded of the Poles, as their price for participating in the alliance, that in event of war the Soviet Union should be allowed to administer a large part of Poland, including Lwów and Wilno (Vilna) – the two largest towns in the eastern half of the country.[7] The Russians also raised the extraordinary question of 'indirect aggression', to which Margot Light alluded. Russia demanded of Britain and France that she should be authorised to intervene in Finland, Estonia and Latvia – not only if the Germans invaded those countries, or in event of a general war against Germany, but also in event of 'indirect aggression'. This term Russia proposed to define as a condition arising in event of 'a reversal of policy in the interest of the aggressor', or in certain other contingencies. Russia herself would presumably be sole judge of whether 'indirect aggression' had taken place. Britain and France were therefore being invited, as the price of an alliance of dubious military value, to acquiesce to Russia doing more or less what she liked in three neutral countries and in half the territory of their own ally.

A sharp difference now arose between Britain and France. The French, whose overriding concern was to keep the Germans out of France at practically any cost, were inclined to agree to the Russian demand; the British, who did not currently fear invasion and could therefore afford to take a more detached and altruistic view of the situation, were divided – the Prime Minister himself firmly opposing acceptance of the Russian definition of 'indirect aggression'. From a 'propaganda' point of view, the British and French Governments were both in a very difficult situation. Naturally they did not wish to advertise a split; while if they had overcome that inhibition and told the world the gravamen of the problem, the effect would have been explosive. Many people who were prepared to support a policy of containing Germany even at risk of war would have had second thoughts if they considered that this containment could only be purchased at the price of authorising Russian aggression. Meanwhile the Baltic states – and perhaps Poland too – would have been driven into Germany's arms. The whole moral force of the Allied case would have been destroyed. As for the Russian alliance which was the immediate objective, any remote possibility which remained would have collapsed amid a welter of furious mutual recriminations.

Whatever people in the British and French Governments may have thought about the 'guarantees' question, they were quite united in the view that an open breakdown in conversations with Russia would have appalling international consequences. While those talks continued, there was always a possibility that an alliance might be effected. If they failed, this would tell Hitler that no alliance need be feared, and would probably precipitate immediate further acts of aggression.

There was one hope of averting a breakdown. The Russians were interested not only in a political agreement but also in a military agreement. While the Westerners argued among themselves whether to yield on 'indirect aggression' or whether some alternative and acceptable formula might perhaps be devised, it was surely useful to go ahead with military conversations. The Russians were delighted with the idea. From the point of view of the West it was important that the military talks should be held because it appeared that Hitler would not strike again while they were in progress and there was some possibility that they might succeed. There was no urgency in those military talks, however, for the overriding object of containing Germany was being achieved so long as they lasted. This may well explain the slow boat, the low rank of the officers and the missing credentials, to which A. J. P. Taylor and Margot Light refer. What ended everything was the Russo-German Non-Aggression Pact, which destroyed any prospect of alliance between Russia and the West, and gave the green light to Hitler.

We may now look behind these faltering relations between

Russia and the West. The real or apparent Soviet designs upon neighbouring countries admit of various possible explanations – some very sinister, other more easily extenuated. Unfortunately the speculations can never be tested against clinching evidence. On certain matters, however, the Soviet point of view was well understood in the West in 1939, and drew considerable sympathy. The Russians had excellent reasons for disliking the three probable Allies. All of them had been involved in the wars of intervention after 1917. The *'cordon sanitaire'* policy persisted long afterwards; indeed, it was still not wholly extinct. Yet it seems unlikely that the Soviet leaders of 1939 believed that Britain, France or Poland had any current designs on the Soviet Union; while they had plenty of reasons for thinking that Germany had many such designs. A very important consideration which undoubtedly still perplexed the Russians was their anxiety to avoid bearing the brunt of whatever fighting might occur. What would happen, say, if Poland were attacked by Germany and soon collapsed under the impact; while the Western Allies hid behind the Maginot Line and the Channel respectively? No doubt it was possible to argue that the mere announcement of a four-power alliance would hold back Germany from war altogether. Perhaps that was true for the time being, but nobody could be sure that it would be true for ever, and Russia could be excused for unwillingness to take the risk.

To a certain degree, the issue between Russia and the existing Allies resolved itself into a matter of confidence in each other's motives, intentions and capacities. Later events have cast much light on the justification or otherwise of the mutual suspicions; but nobody could know about that for certain in the middle of 1939. Important as this record of explicit suspicions and past hostility was, there is a strong argument for the view that an even more serious difficulty lay in the fact that the Western countries on one side and the Soviet Union on the other knew very little of each other's thought processes, and in consequence usually suspected the worst. As we have already seen, there was a great deal of misunderstanding between Britain, France and Poland, who shared considerable elements of a common cultural and diplomatic tradition; it was perhaps inevitable from the start that any attempt to establish an alliance with Soviet Russia, whose outlook was so radically different, would founder on the rock of mutual incomprehension, if on no other.

A different aspect of the situation would later prove of vital importance. Was there a third option open to Russia as well as the familiar possibilities of four-power alliance and grumbling neutrality: the option of a deal with Germany? The existence of this possibility was recognised by some people in the West as far back as the spring of 1939,[8] but there is little indication that it was properly thought through. Most people either omitted it from their minds altogether, or discounted it because both Nazis and Communists made the loudest possible ideological noises in execration of each other's regimes. Subsequent experience would show that preoccupation with ideology rather than *Realpolitik* led the Allies into a very gross omission from their calculations.

We may extenuate this omission to some degree because of the large part which ideology was currently playing in the popular politics of the West. Donald Watt has written about the 'Popular Front' movements which, in one way or another, greatly influenced the thought of many people who were by no means Communists, but would have considered themselves Democratic Socialists, Liberals or even Conservatives. Those people were generally disposed in all matters to set the best possible construction on actions of the Soviet Union.

This pro-Russian sentiment, like the pro-German sentiment which touched a different body of people, was influenced by a vague sense of collective guilt for past sins. It profoundly affected reactions to current events. When negotiations between Russia and the West ran into very evident difficulties in the summer of 1939, a great many people in the West took it as almost axiomatic that any fault lay with the British and French Governments. Those Governments, in their turn, were still wrestling with the task of securing if possible an acceptable agreement with Russia and, as we have seen, could not explain the true reasons for delay. In France – where the Communists returned over seventy deputies and had much trade union support – recriminations over failure to accommodate Russia were particularly noisy; but very raucous voices were also raised on the other side of the controversy. These were inspired in part at least by real fear of a Communist take-over in France itself.

The fierce and conflicting emotions which Russia aroused in other countries made it certain that the Russo-German Non-Aggression Pact of 23 August 1939 would throw all countries and all calculations into confusion. For a few days, people had the greatest difficulty in taking their bearings. When they recovered from the shock, most people in the West decided that the pact constituted a wanton act of selfish perfidy by the Soviet Union, which turned a Second World War from a likelihood to a certainty. As more facts were revealed in the ensuing days, the pact was perceived as part of a cynical carve-up between Hitler and Stalin, whereby Russia greatly extended her territory and sphere of influence, and simultaneously embroiled Germany and the West in war. Such assessments of the situation were at least as common among people on the democratic 'left' as among people on the 'right'. Very rapid and fundamental reappraisals were necessary in other quarters too. Italy and Japan, partners with Germany in the 'Anti-Comintern Pact', cooled perceptibly in their developing affections towards the Nazis. Few people guessed how matters would eventually turn out between Russia and Germany.

Lothar Kettenacker invites us also to look at matters from the German angle. This is the most difficult, and in one sense the most important, to understand. All nations contain their share of violent lunatics. Germany was no exception, and it is not difficult to understand how activities like Jew-baiting and aggressive war appealed to such people. During the war itself, and for a short period afterwards, there prevailed in Allied countries the astonishing view that Germans were in some mysterious way different from other people, possessing an exceptional ingredient of original sin. That view, like all racialist attitudes, seems so monstrously absurd in retrospect that it is now difficult to realise that apparently sensible people ever entertained it; yet the historian is obliged to tell us that many of them manifestly did. When we seek a more credible explanation, the facile answers frequently advanced do not seem satisfactory. It is not enough to reply that the Gestapo was ubiquitous, that concentration camps yawned for victims and Dr Goebbels was skilled at his job. The Germans did not, in the event, behave like people who had been dragooned into action exclusively by terror of their own government and false information about other people, though such considerations no doubt played their part.

The task of Lothar Kettenacker in presenting the German view becomes peculiarly difficult because so little has been written since the war in extenuation or even in explanation of what the view of ordinary Germans may have been. The world has been so sickened by the horrors of the extermination camps that not enough attention has been given to a very serious problem: why so many apparently decent Germans were prepared to go along with Hitler so far. Dr Kettenacker draws our attention to the doubts which many Germans undeniably felt about the direction in which they were being led. The British Government was fully conscious of such doubts: indeed, the leaflet raids upon Germany in the first few days of war suggest that Britain was disposed to exaggerate rather than to underrate their importance. Yet as the war developed most Germans behaved very much as most Britons and Poles behaved: as people who believed in the necessity and righteousness of what they were doing. There was little sign of that neutralism, or even active support for the declared national enemy, which affected large numbers of people in France, the Soviet Union, Italy and some of the smaller countries on both sides of the great divide.

In our own century, well within the lifetimes and memories of many of us, the existence of hundreds of millions of people was dominated for years by the Second World War and its aftermath; and tens of millions of those people died in the struggle. No good will be done by eulogising or condemning men of that time; but if we try to understand their behaviour we may — who knows? — derive some ideas about how to prevent a repetition of the catastrophe.

## NOTES AND REFERENCES

1. Anna M. Cienciala, *Poland and the Western Powers 1938–1939* (London and Toronto, 1968).
2. A. Adamthwaite, *France and the Coming of the Second World War 1936–1939* (London, 1977).
3. I. D. Colvin, *The Chamberlain Cabinet* . . . (London, 1971).
4. S. K. Newman, *March 1939: The British Guarantee to Poland* (Oxford, 1976).
5. Neville to Hilda Chamberlain, 2 April 1939, NC 18/1/1092, University of Birmingham Library.
6. Ibid.
7. See, for example, Dalton diary, 22 August 1939, British Library of Economic Science, LSE.
8. See, for example, Hore-Belisha's views on 3 May 1939, Cabinet 26(39), CAB 23/98, Public Record Office.

# Select Bibliography

This bibliography is based upon books recommended by the contributors. It is designed merely to suggest further reading, and is not intended as a comprehensive list of source material. As several titles are relevant to more than one chapter, it has not been divided according to the particular contributions.

Adamthwaite, A. (1977) *France and the Coming of the Second World War, 1936–1939* (London).

Aster, Sidney (1973) *The Making of the Second World War* (London).

Beaufré, André (1965) *Le Drame de 1940* (Paris).

Bédarida, François (1979) *Le Stratégie secrète de la drôle de guerre* (Paris).

Bialer, Seweryn, (ed.)(1970) *Stalin and His Generals: Soviet Military Memoirs of World War II* (London).

Bonnet, Georges (1964–8) *Défense de la paix*, 2 vols (Geneva).

Bracher, Karl (1969) *Die Deutsche Diktatur* (Köln).

Bregmen, Aleksander (1974) *Najlepszy sojusnik Hitlers* (*Hitler's Best Ally*) 4th edn (London).

Cairns, John C. (1974) 'Some Recent Historians and the "Strange Defeat" of 1940', *Journal of Modern History*, vol. 46, March.

Calvacoressi, Peter, and Guy Wint (1972) *Total War* (London).

Chapman, Guy (1968) *Why France Collapsed* (London).

Chivaidze, A. D. (1976) *Angliskii kabinet nakanune vtoroi mirovoi voiny* (Tbilisi).

Churchill, Winston S. (1948 *et seq.*) *The Second World War:* vol. 1, *The Gathering Storm*; vol. 2 *The Twilight War* (London).

Cienciala, Anna Maria (1968) *Poland and the Western Powers 1938–1939* (London and Toronto).

Colvin, I. D. (1971) *The Chamberlain Cabinet . . .* (London).

Cowling, Maurice (1975) *The Impact of Hitler: 1933–1940.* (London).

Daladier, E. (1977) *La France sous le gouvernement Daladier* (Colloque: Fondation Nationale des Sciences Politiques).

*Documents on Polish–Soviet Relations 1939–1945* (1961) vols I and II (London).

Deist, Wilhelm *et al.* (eds) (1979) *Das Deutsche Reich und der Zweite Weltkrieg* (Stuttgart).

Douglas, Roy (1977) *In the Year of Munich* (London).

Douglas, Roy (1978) *The Advent of War, 1939–1940* (London).

Duroselle, J.-B. (1979) *La Décadence, 1932–1939* (Paris).

Ehrman, John (1956) *Grand Strategy* (London).

Fest, Joachim C. (1973) *Hitler* (Frankfurt/Main and Berlin;  London, 1977).

Foot, Michael and Donald Bruce (1949) *Who are the Patriots?* (London).

Gilbert, Martin (1976) *Winston S. Churchill*, vol. 5 (London).

Gilbert, Martin and R. Gott (1963) *The Appeasers* (London).

Grechko, A. A. *et al.* (eds) (1974) *Istoriya vtoroi mirovoi voiny*, vols 2 and 3 (Moscow).

Gromyko, A.A. *et al.* (eds) (1965, 1975) *Istoriya diplomatii* (Moscow), 2nd ed. of vol. 3, 1965; 2nd ed of vol. 4, 1975.

Henke, Josef (1973) *England in Hitlers politischem Kalkül 1935–1939* (Boppard).

Hildebrand, Klaus (1976) *Deutsche Außenpolitik 1933–1945*, 3rd edn (Stuttgart).

Hildebrand, Klaus (1979) *Das Dritte Reich* (München).

Hofer, W. (1955) *War Premeditated* (London).

Howard, Michael (1972) *The Continental Commitment* (London).

Inglis, Brian (1971) *Abdication* (Geneva).

Johnson, Douglas (1972) 'Britain and France in 1940', *Transactions of the Royal Historical Society*, vol. 22.

Keynes, J. Maynard (Lord Keynes) (1919) *The Economic Consequences of the Peace* (London).

Le Goyet, Pierre (1976) *Le mystère Gamelin* (Paris).

Maisky, I. M. (1964) *Who Helped Hitler?* (London).

*Maly Rocznik Statystyczny 1931–9 (Pocket Year-Book of Statistics)* (1940) (London).

Michalka, Wolfgang (1980) *Ribbentrop und die deutsche Weltpolitik 1933–1940* (München).

Muggeridge, Malcolm (1940) *The Thirties* (London).

Namier, Sir Lewis (1948) *Diplomatic Prelude* (London).

*New Times* (supplement to), February 1948, no. 8.

Newman, S. K. (1976) *March 1939: the British Guarantee to Poland* (Oxford).

Noël, Léon (1946) *L'Agression allemande contre la Pologne* (Paris).

*Official Documents concerning Polish–German and Polish–Soviet Relations 1933–1939* (1940) (The Polish White Book) (London).

Peden, G. C. (1979) *British Rearmament and the Treasury, 1932–1939* (Edinburgh).

Petrov, Vladimir (ed.) (1968) *'22 June 1941': Soviet Historians and the German Invasion* (Columbia, S.C.).

Polonsky, Antony (1972) *Politics in Independent Poland 1921–1939* (London).

Polonsky, Antony (1976) *The Great Powers and the Polish Question* (London).

Ponomaryov, B. N. and A. A. Gromyko (1969) *History of Soviet Foreign Policy 1917–45* (Moscow).

Raczyński, Edward (1948) *The British–Polish Alliance: its Origin and Meaning* (London).

Renouvin, Pierre (1958) *Histoire des relations internationales: les crises du XX siècle, VIII. 1929–45* (Paris).

Rich, Norman (1973–4) *Hitler's War Aims*, 2 vols (London).

Spier, E (1963) *Focus: a footnote to the History of the Thirties* (London).

Stachura, P. D. (ed) (1978) *The Shaping of the Nazi State* (London).

Taylor, A. J. P. (1965) *English History 1914–1945* (Oxford).

Taylor, A. J. P. (1961) *Origins of the Second World War* (Harmondsworth).

Taylor, Telford (1979) *Munich: the Price of Peace* (London).

Thorne, Christopher (1972) *The Limits of Foreign Policy: the West, the League and the Far Eastern Crisis of 1931–1933* (London).

Toscano, Mario (1967) *The Origins of the Pact of Steel*, 2nd edn (Baltimore).

Watt, Donald C. (1975) *Too Serious a Business: European Armed Forces and the Approach to the Second World War* (London).

Wendt, Jörgen W. (1971) *Economic Appeasement: Handel und Finanzen in der britischen Deutschlandpolitik 1933–1939* (Düsseldorf).

Young, Robert J. (1978) *In Command of France* (Cambridge, Mass. and London).

Zhilin, P. A. (1978) *The Second World War and Our Time* (Moscow).

# Index